ADVANCE PRAISE

"Dr. Bader has created an engaging and valuable tool for parents to enhance their young child's brain development through music. And no music background is necessary to use this excellent resource."

—LAURY CHRISTIE, MM, DISTINGUISHED EMERITA PROFESSOR OF MUSIC, UNIVERSITY OF SOUTH CAROLINA

"*Music for the Developing Brain* is a highly practical guide to helping children connect with vital aspects of music and music-making in a natural and fun way. Sound pedagogical principles relating to sequential learning—as well as to such fundamental musical concepts as pitch and rhythm—lay important groundwork for future study. This is an invaluable resource for all who are interested in nurturing their child's innate propensity toward music comprehension and enjoyment."

—STEPHEN TAYLOR, DMA, FORMER MUSIC DEPARTMENT CHAIR OF THE SOUTH CAROLINA GOVERNOR'S SCHOOL FOR THE ARTS AND HUMANITIES

"Dr. Bader provides an engaging approach to fostering musical growth as a comfortable and natural part of a child's development...This accessible book allows parents to support their children and learn alongside them with step-by-step guidance. Parents who may already be engaging in similar activities with their babies and toddlers can learn how being more intentional in their musical/rhythmic playtime can reap lasting benefits while helping to form warm parent-child relationships."

— DEBORAH A. RUTH, BM, NCTM, OWNER & INSTRUCTOR OF RUTH PIANO STUDIO IN LEXINGTON, SOUTH CAROLINA

"As an educator of elementary school children for over a quarter of a century with no music education or training, I found this book engaging, clear to understand, and easy to implement. I highly recommend this asset for classroom teachers and homeschooling parents who want to enrich their curriculum with sound musical principles."

— MARY ANN WHEELER, MED IN ADMINISTRATION AND SUPERVISION, FORMER PRINCIPAL

"*Music for the Developing Brain* makes the science of brain development affordable and practical to parents, teachers, and caregivers. Dr. Bader takes complex research in neuroscience and translates it into everyday, joyful activities; her program incorporates music as part of natural parenting, teaching, and learning together with young children. Please read her introduction—you'll be fascinated and want to learn more."

—JANET WATKINS JENDRON, BOARD PRESIDENT, NURTURINGS.ORG

"Dr. Bader's time, experience, and big heart were put into this book, and every page shows her love for music. Coming from a musical background and being the father of four young children, this book has given me guidelines to teach my children the joy of having music in our lives."

—NICK RUGGIERO, DMD, PROSTHODONTIST AND FATHER OF FOUR YOUNG CHILDREN

"Dr. Bader's book is a delightful approach to introducing music to babies (even prenatally) and young children... If music is indeed the 'universal language,' we all benefit when families see the importance of having music and art in our lives...I highly recommend this book."

—BARBARA NICHOLSON, MED, CEIM, CO-FOUNDER OF NURTURINGS.COM, CO-AUTHOR OF *ATTACHED AT THE HEART: EIGHT PRINCIPLES TO RAISING CONNECTED AND COMPASSIONATE CHILDREN*

"At the core of Dr. Jane Bader's teaching is the truth that being human means being musical. Through her book, she helps us discover that each person has innate senses of rhythm and pitch. Music is human expression and communication. By tapping into these universal senses throughout *Music for the Developing Brain*, Dr. Bader is able to teach anyone how to make music, from infants to elders. With this beautiful guide, parents and children can go on a musical journey together."

—EMILY GINDLESPARGER, *WSJ* BESTSELLING BOOK COACH AND AUTHOR OF *PLEASE MAKE ME LOVE ME*

"In the over thirty years that I have known Dr. Bader, I have watched her dedication to improving the ease with which children can play and enjoy music. She is absolutely passionate and committed to sharing her expertise with all those who are invested in children and actually making the process fun and easy."

—PATRICIA CANNON, MSN, RN, VICE PRESIDENT OF HIS INTERNATIONAL, INC.

"Dr. Bader has developed a fascinating and fun approach to teaching musical concepts to preschoolers—and the teacher doesn't have to be a trained musician or educator! This could be a very valuable and popular resource."

—GORDON (DICK) GOODWIN, DMA, DISTINGUISHED PROFESSOR EMERITUS OF COMPOSITION AT THE UNIVERSITY OF SOUTH CAROLINA

"*Music for the Developing Brain*'s insightful psychological perspective will guide students of all ages...whether your goal is mastering performance, teaching, or learning the art of improvisation."

—NANDO PELUSI, PHD, CBT CLINICAL PSYCHOLOGIST AND PROFESSIONAL MUSICIAN

"Dr. Bader's breadth of learning leaps at the reader, yet her prose is gentle, understanding, and compassionate towards the novice...I recommend this book to all who wish to support a child's cognitive development through music, and in life at large."

—DAN L. TROTTER, PHD, JD-MBA, MA, AUTHOR OF *REDNECK IN RED CHINA: AN AMERICAN SOUTHERNER'S LIFE IN MODERN CHINA*

Music
for the
Developing Brain

A SIMPLE, AT-HOME PROGRAM

JANE J. BADER, DMA

NeuroMusicNotes
MEDIA

Hardcover ISBN: 979-8-9897291-0-4
Paperback ISBN: 979-8-9897291-1-1
Ebook ISBN: 979-8-9897291-3-5

Images by Marie Catherine Burton on pages 43, 44, 77, 79, 80, 81, 83, 85, 99, 102, 103 and 129.

Illustrations by Joyce Elizabeth Burton on page 122.

Disclaimer
The purpose of this book is to help parents and caregivers guide their children's music education. Parents and caregivers should expect progress if they are following the program as directed; however, all children learn at different paces and in different ways. Please be patient with your children, and remember that learning depends on each child's brain development and should occur naturally as part of their normal growth and development. There is no guarantee that your child will attain a specific level of musical or academic achievement.

This book is not a product of artificial intelligence (AI) in any way. Permission to submit any content for future AI is not given now or at any time.

When reading any research results, one must remember that correlation does not equal causation. There may be an association, but the actual cause may not be specifically identified; however, there can be value in observing common occurrences.

This book is dedicated to my family,
who have worked tirelessly, cheerfully sharing
their talents and abilities, and encouraged me
every step of the way!

TABLE OF CONTENTS

List of Illustrations

LIST OF MUSICAL ACTIVITIES

FOREWORD

Congratulations on purchasing this valuable book to help you guide your children's journey into the world of music! This book will help you teach them about music and how to experience music. The good news is that you don't have to be musical or have musical training yourself. You just have to be interested in your child and encourage their study of music. At an early age, music is learned by exposure, and you can provide this exposure to your child using the strategies contained in this book.

As a music education researcher in the area of parental involvement in musical development, I have observed powerful evidence that parents, as their child's first teachers, have an important role to play in the development of their child's musical skills, musical knowledge, and attitudes about music study. Benjamin Bloom, in his book, *Developing Talent in Young People*, includes a chapter on musical development that documents the importance of early home musical environments that nurture musical development, establish good practice habits, and support study skills that translate to other areas of learning. Early exposure increases the child's musical potential, and as your child gets older, your involvement in their musical development will sustain their interest in music for a lifetime of musical enjoyment.

Dr. Bader has written a valuable book that will be useful for parents of preschool children who are starting music. As her former dissertation advisor, I know that Dr. Bader has both the practical pedagogical experience and the scholarly background to speak on this subject with great authority. She is a superb piano pedagogue with a great understanding of how children learn music using the natural pathways for music found in our brains.

Stephen F. Zdzinski, PhD
Professor of Music Education
Frost School of Music
University of Miami

INTRODUCTION

When my mother was a child, she wanted so badly to learn to play the piano that she pretended to play on the edge of the kitchen table. She grew up during the Great Depression, and her family could not even afford food, so there was no possible way for her dream to come true.

She promised herself that she would get an education by earning scholarships and follow up by finding a good job, and she did. After I was born, my parents utilized their strong work ethic to provide opportunities for me that they did not have as children, and I am humbled and profoundly grateful.

Human beings are designed to be musical; the only difference is that some are trained, and others are untrained.

Can you:
- hum or sing along with music?
- tap your foot in rhythm with songs on your playlist?
- dance or move in rhythm to what you hear?
- sing a recognizable "Happy Birthday"?

If you answered "yes" to any of these questions, then you are well on the way to becoming a musician and teaching your child how to become a musician, too!

Most parents and caregivers want to provide the best possible education for their children, but many do not have any significant experience in learning or teaching music. Maybe you wish that your parents had been able to provide you with music lessons. Perhaps you want your children to grow up with the benefit of learning music but do not have the time or budget to enroll them in music classes for babies, toddlers, and preschoolers.

I have some great news: this book is written for you!

Music is a universal language, so I have removed many financial barriers to provide truly inclusive music education. The only things you will need are some 3" × 5" index cards, a pencil and a marker, internet access, and (eventually) a small, electronic piano keyboard. My simple, at-home program empowers parents and caregivers with no prior musical training to enjoy musical activities with their young children (ages 0–5) while enhancing their children's brain development.

Making music is a complex process: when musicians play, they usually read the written notes on the page, hear mentally how the notes should sound, produce the sound physically, and listen in order to make corrections in real time as necessary. This type of learning can affect both the size and efficiency of different parts of the brain, particularly in processing sound, acquiring language, listening, reading, and learning mathematics.

Researchers continue to study how music training can affect brain structure and function, as well as how the development of these skills during childhood can have a positive influence on a person's life through older adulthood. If you want to know more about the research results and implications of neuroscience as it relates to music study and performance, please go to Suggested Reading at the end of the book. My music education program is based on an enormous body of research and observations, combined with my own formal education, experience, and observations.

I have earned a Bachelor of Science in Cell Biology, a Certificate and Registration in Medical Technology, a Master of Music, and a Doctor of Musical Arts in Piano Pedagogy (PED uh go jee) with a secondary concentration in Composition. Pedagogy is usually understood as the science of teaching. The emphasis of my academic research has been on sequencing: how the order in which a subject is learned contributes to the overall understanding and absorption of material. In particular, I have focused on how learning music can be accomplished as a natural part of children's growth and development. Consequently, I am able to combine science and music in order to create special learning experiences for parents, caregivers, and their young children.

As a marine biology researcher and medical laboratory manager, I have obtained decades of experience in making and recording observations, as well as in reading and understanding scientific literature. As an award-winning composer, I can write and arrange music to serve nearly any teaching need, and it is a privilege to share some of my songs and pieces with you. Finally, as a mother, grandmother, homeschooling veteran, and former professor, I have extensive experience observing how children, teenagers, and adults learn and then figuring out ways to make learning both easier and more enjoyable.

This book is designed to show parents and caregivers how to include a simple, step-by-step music learning process in their daily lives so that learning occurs as part of their children's normal growth and development. Musical sounds can be used to express a purpose or emotion. During the process, you will learn about rhythm, pitch, dynamics, tempo, articulation, timbre (TAM bur), and expression—all considered as concepts of music or musical concepts. You'll be introduced to the layout and sound of the keyboard, as well as to how music is represented visually.

These activities are planned to be completed within a child's limited attention span, and they can be a fun alternative to screen time. Many of the activities take 5 minutes or less and can be done easily while waiting for coffee to brew or popcorn to pop, while in daycare or school lines, or while getting dressed.

While you are preparing for and doing these activities, please check to be sure that your environment is safe and that you do not do anything that is physically uncomfortable for you and your children. Hearing protection is very important, so keep the volume only loud enough to be heard accurately. Remember to clear a space on the floor that is free of toys and other objects so that you will have room to move freely.

Unlike some other books about child development, everyone should start at the very beginning of this book, no matter what age your child is. The concepts and activities are in a particular order designed to make them easier to learn. Read gradually so that you won't feel overwhelmed, and as we go along, I will explain how and why I teach the way I do.

You can move on when skills are accomplished easily. Some children absorb concepts of music quickly, and others need more time. One reason that I usually do not include specific ages along the way is that I don't want to create unreasonable expectations or limit children's potential for learning. This approach allows freedom to learn without the pressure of completing a certain amount of material by a definite time. Occasionally, I might mention an age at which the majority of children are able to complete a specific activity; however, it is simply an observation, not an expected milestone.

Most children will learn the skills in this book by the time they are ready to begin elementary school, but it is never too late to begin learning concepts of music. Just start at the beginning and adapt the activities to match the abilities of your older children. You might even engage them in creating new activities that can show their understanding of each concept by seeing, hearing, and doing.

This book will not teach you to actually play pieces from written music, but you will be introduced to foundational concepts while you and your children enjoy making music together. If you practice five days a week, following the directions in the book and the demonstrations on my YouTube channel, you should expect your child to learn to recognize, name, and describe sounds they hear, and eventually to play melodies of simple songs by the time they are ready for elementary school.

By the end of the book, all of you should be prepared to continue music study if you want to. Even if no one does, you can be satisfied that you have provided a valuable learning experience for both yourself and your children.

Are you ready to get started? Let's take the first step together and begin our musical journey!

Chapter 1

Our baby kicked in rhythm to music with a strong beat before she was born! When my husband and I were expecting our daughter, both of us played in a band. He played alto saxophone, and I played keyboard, so she was exposed to live music at church as well as when we practiced at home. Most babies are born after approximately nine months of development that includes listening to the mother's heartbeat, which is normally a steady beat and is repeated continually. They can feel rhythm, even though they cannot articulate the concept, and have been observed to be able to tell when a downbeat is missing or is not in the expected place. In addition, there is evidence that they can distinguish between a familiar song and an unfamiliar one as early as two weeks before birth. If you'd like to read more about these topics, look up Winkler and Hepper, respectively, in Suggested Reading.

Before we go on, I want you to know how much I wish I could be there in person to guide and encourage you during these challenging years of parenting. Now that I have the perspective that arrives when your children become adults and have children of their own, I realize how important the cumulative effect of daily activities can be. As a mom, I juggled homeschooling our daughter, taking two doctoral courses each semester, teaching piano, participating in church activities (including composing, arranging, rehearsing, and performing music), and driving her to piano and violin lessons, orchestra rehearsals, and field trips, as well as her volunteer responsibilities at a state park. Our daughter thrived on many activities and liked to keep busy with things that she enjoyed, so we simply followed her lead.

If you want your children to experience the benefits of learning musical concepts, you, too, can learn how to help them discover rhythm, pitch, and more through simple activities. It is never too early to explore music with your children. This book can help parents and caregivers learn how to encourage and guide their children's musical development during the years before music lessons are ever considered. All of the activities are designed for parents and caregivers with little time and can provide meaningful ways to connect with children while nurturing their growth and development. As a bonus, parents and caregivers can also experience musical concepts through enjoyable activities along with their children as they grow.

It is important not to place limits on children's accomplishments, especially when they are younger. Children grow and learn a tremendous amount between birth and age 5, and their brains and little bodies are capable of doing amazing things!

MUSIC AND BRAIN DEVELOPMENT

Many studies have shown that musical achievement can be related to academic performance. Researchers are also studying the impact that learning music has on how children develop an understanding of their world and acquire thinking skills. According to studies by Leipold and others in Suggested Reading, being a musician can have noticeable effects on both the structure and function of neural networks in the brain. The connection between the two hemispheres of the brain was found to be larger in musicians, particularly in children who began studying music before the age of 8. To learn more, look up Schlaug and others in Suggested Reading.

BENEFITS OF MUSIC STUDY

There can be many benefits of studying music, based on extensive observation, that go far beyond learning to play a piece, such as promoting brain development and nurturing life skills during the process. Here is a list of some ways that music study can influence academic, social, physical, and personal development:

Academic Development
- Understanding and following directions
- Keeping up with materials
- Listening to verbal directions
- Using an expanded vocabulary
- Developing attention to detail
- Promoting memory skills
- Enhancing understanding of math concepts, especially fractions

Social Development

- Being patient with others as well as oneself
- Developing social skills
- Respecting others
- Learning humility
- Coping with expectations of others
- Learning to accept imperfection
- Developing confidence
- Developing perseverance
- Pursuing excellence rather than perfection
- Learning to work with others and get along with them
- Preparing for job interviews by participating in auditions and recitals

Physical Development

- Developing physical coordination
- Developing large muscle movement
- Developing fine motor skills
- Providing physical activity
- Improving posture and core strength
- Learning healthy habits of repetitive motion

Personal Development: Self-Regulation

- Setting priorities
- Managing time
- Developing initiative
- Setting and achieving realistic goals
- Developing organizational skills
- Delaying gratification

- Learning self-discipline
- Developing personal responsibility
- Developing a personal work ethic
- Lengthening one's attention span
- Deriving satisfaction from one's accomplishments

Making music is a complex process: remember that when musicians play, they usually read the written notes on the page, hear mentally how the notes should sound, produce the sound physically, and listen in order to make corrections in real time as necessary. In addition, there must be an underlying pulse with strong and weak beats. Add another person playing, and musicians have to expand their listening to include a part that they do not see or play, requiring them to hear their individual sounds as part of a whole. The complexity increases with each additional musician added to the group, usually called an ensemble (ahn SAHM buhl). I have great respect for marching band directors, in particular, because they teach not only how to play different musical instruments skillfully, but also how to march in intricate patterns at the same time. This is a huge workout for the brain!

Many children who have studied music can be able to understand math more easily, especially fractions. This possible advantage may be due to the division of the beat into equal parts: usually halves, fourths, or thirds. History provides examples of mathematicians and scientists who were also musicians—as early as Pythagoras, an Ancient Greek philosopher; and as recently as Albert Einstein, Brian May of "Queen," Art Garfunkel of "Simon & Garfunkel," and Phil Alvin of "The Blasters."

HOW TO ENCOURAGE CHILDREN DURING MUSIC STUDY

It is important early in life to celebrate children's efforts that contribute to all of their accomplishments. Notice that I did not say to wait until the results happen. If you are a parent with an older child, do you remember when they took a step for the first time? Did you clap your hands, smile brightly, and say, "Yay—you did it!"? You were likely rewarded with a big smile from your child, too, as they promptly plopped onto the floor.

When you think about it, growing up is a constant process of learning new skills necessary to survive and thrive among others. It is important to understand that the harder you work, the better you get. As parents and caregivers, we have an enormous responsibility because children depend on us to provide an example of effective adulthood and to celebrate the effort that makes their successes possible.

HOW TO EXPRESS PRAISE

Focus on the child's efforts and resulting accomplishments instead of their talent or intelligence. The reason is that if a young child hears that they are smart or talented, they may expect things to happen easily. Because playing an instrument is a skill and not only an intellectual pursuit, effort is required for repetition in order to learn. No one is born knowing how to play an instrument; everyone has to learn from the very beginning. Although it may be easier for some, effort is still required. Following a proper sequence of learning musical concepts can give children a foundation to make it easier for future study.

EARLY CHILDHOOD EXPERIENCES WITH MUSIC

Before and after birth, our daughter was exposed to music both at home and at church. At 6 weeks old, she could differentiate among songs I would play for her; it was easy to tell because she would stop crying when I played a particular song. Singing was part of many daily activities, although it did not seem to help while getting her into a car seat! When she was a toddler, we took her to some informal performances. She also learned many children's songs, and I made up songs on a number of occasions.

At age 3, she began a class in creative movement, in which the children learned to move their bodies in a certain way in rhythm with the music. They practiced each week and connected different motions. By the end of the semester, they were able to remember them in order for the recital. She enjoyed this class and continued for three years.

When our daughter was 5, my husband and I asked her if she would like to learn to play the piano. Her formal piano instruction began only after she expressed a desire to learn. The reason we asked her opinion was that many times prospective students and parents have arrived at an interview because the parent wanted to learn to play the piano, not the child. Often, children will develop the necessary fine motor coordination between 4 and 6, although their attention span may be short.

Our daughter learned to play the piano as well as read music in a straightforward manner. At age 6, she wanted to add violin. Both piano and violin included group activities. We allotted 20–30 total minutes of practice for each instrument at least five days a week; however, the cumulative time each day included focused segments of no more than 10–15 minutes, with some as few as 5. Focusing for even a short period of time is more effective than spending more time mindlessly going through the motions.

Every day, we eagerly anticipated her "performances" and said something along these lines:

- "Is it time for your recital yet?"
- "When are you going to play for us?"
- "What are you planning to play for us today?"
- "Ooh—a concert!"

When she would finish, we would clap and provide positive reinforcement specifically about her efforts, and we would thank her for sharing her music with us. Were we acting or being hypocritical? Absolutely not! We had the pleasure of watching our child learn through growth and development, which was a major parenting objective, so we enjoyed encouraging her during the process as she became more and more successful. When the time came for formal recitals, she learned her pieces well in advance and practiced actually performing them. Consequently, she always enjoyed giving an excellent performance.

Performing in front of an audience can be a wonderful experience to cultivate for a young child. It's a win-win situation: even if they do something different, they're so cute, anyway—and no one expects perfection, particularly at that age. The important thing is that they learn to enjoy sharing their accomplishments with others and receive applause and commendation for doing so. The experience that these performances provide is especially useful later in life during job interviews!

Although it may seem far-fetched, children can display talent at an early age. Celine Tam of Hong Kong began learning to sing at age 3 and sang in public at age 4. She appeared on *America's Got Talent* in 2017, at the age of 9, and was awarded the Golden Buzzer, thus advancing directly to the semifinals.

Another performer on YouTube is listed as 4 years old and shows both an excellent and mature understanding of music. It is possible to teach young children to play intricate pieces by extensive imitation and repetition; however, this child actually gives an expressive musical performance.

Another example is Roberta Battaglia, whose parents described how she could actually sing on pitch at just 13 months old. When asked how and when she started performing, she said she began when she was 3½ years old. Her father was a sound engineer, and when the microphone was left on the floor, she would pick it up and sing "Twinkle, Twinkle Little Star." Seven years later, in 2020, she was performing on an enormous stage for the entire world on *America's Got Talent*. In fact, she had her eleventh birthday just days before the final competition and came in fourth!

D'Corey Johnson of Louisville, Kentucky, not only sings but also loves acting, dancing, and playing the piano. His mother said that he began humming the songs at St. Stephen's Baptist Church before he could talk and was singing in choir at age 4. At age 9, he sang the national anthem for his school, Bates

Elementary, and a video posted by his principal went viral.

I have selected some videos on YouTube to provide examples of childhood performances. Please go to my website, DrJaneJBader.com/chapter-videos, to begin the playlist for Chapter 1. Sometimes, videos are removed on YouTube, so if you find that one is missing, please send an email to me at Jane@DrJaneJBader.com with the subject line "Missing Video." It would help if you could include the video's title and the chapter in which the missing video is located. I would really appreciate it!

Like everything else with childhood, there is no guarantee that children will be able to achieve similar accomplishments; however, right now, the best thing you can do for your child's musical development is to provide enjoyable ways to explore music together. Repeat, repeat, and then repeat some more. Young children usually can tolerate much more repetition than adults, so keep going and going beyond the point you feel comfortable, as long as they enjoy the activities. Remember to review what you have already learned because all of the activities combine to build a foundation necessary for future learning experiences.

Are you ready to go on a wonderful, musical adventure with me that can also enhance your child's brain development? Let's go!

Chapter 2

Are you wondering why we start learning music with sounds instead of books? Think about how babies learn language. They listen and learn to make sounds, which become syllables. Those syllables then become words, phrases, sentences, paragraphs, chapters, and eventually large papers or books. Would you expect children to learn to read books before they could talk and know what words mean? Of course not. At the appropriate developmental time, children normally learn to speak, read, and write in their native language through listening and responding while they are with their family, caregivers, and others. In a similar way, reading music can be introduced after children have already absorbed a vocabulary of sound through experiences.

SEQUENCING: SOUND BEFORE SIGHT

Why do so many music lesson books begin with the mechanics of learning to read music? How can learning be accomplished as a natural course of events? I was intrigued enough by these questions to devote nineteen months of my life to researching how to make learning easier and more enjoyable for children as well as parents and caregivers. The process that I focused on is known among educators as sequencing: how the order of learning a subject influences a student's understanding. Sequencing can work across the spectrum of all academic subjects. In fact, we used it effectively in homeschooling to move from concepts to details with great success.

What did I learn? Our society is primarily visual, and most teaching methods are focused on children who can already read and understand words. The important thing for me was that I explored how to make musical growth a natural part of child development so that learning occurs by experiences and understanding rather than memorization of formal definitions. This process works for adults as well, enabling parents, caregivers, and children to discover a truly creative subject: how to enjoy making music. If you'd like to read more about these topics, look up Cassidy and Speer; Flowers; Nyberg, Habib, McIntosh, and Tulving; and Wheeler, Petersen, and Buckner in Suggested Reading.

ORAL COMMUNICATION AND MUSIC

Have you noticed your baby trying to communicate with you? Yes, babies do learn words, but they start with syllables that are usually called babble. The first time I heard our grandson babble, I responded by repeating back to him what he had said. A look of utter delight came over his little face, and he promptly babbled another pattern. When I repeated that one, he looked like it had totally made his day. I know it certainly did mine!

There is a connection between learning language and music because the same brain systems are used for both: one for memorizing words, meanings, and tunes, and the other for absorbing grammar as well as harmony. If you want to know more, look up the article by Ullman in Suggested Reading. The optimum sequence is the same for both: listening, making sounds first, responding, increasing complexity, and repeating.

♪ MUSICAL ACTIVITY: BABBLE WITH PITCH

When your baby babbles, mirror the sounds in response by saying "bah," like you are having a conversation. Notice the variations in high and low sounds and respond similarly.

♪ MUSICAL ACTIVITY: BABBLE WITH RHYTHM

Next, listen closely and feel the rhythm of the babble. This time, say "bah" in a similar pattern. Even if there are only two or three syllables, converse with the baby. Change the consonants and vowels when appropriate.

♪ MUSICAL ACTIVITY: RHYTHMIC PATTERNS WITH PERCUSSION INSTRUMENTS

If it is too early for the baby to clap, you can use a teether with attached bells for this activity. Be sure that this toy is constructed safely for the baby's age. Observe as your baby shakes the toy. Is the shaking a steady beat, or is it a pattern? Respond to the baby in a similar way. If you have two toys that make sounds, you can use one to respond in the same rhythm. That way, you can switch toys when the baby wants yours.

Perhaps you would like to make an adult percussion instrument for you to play by combining some keys on a ring to shake, tapping an aluminum pie pan with your fingertips, or placing some dried beans, rice, or something similar into a small leftover container with a secured lid. Unless you have child-proofed your instrument, the most important thing is to keep yours away from the baby for safety.

HOW TO EXPERIENCE PITCH AND RHYTHM

Have you ever listened to a tune and found yourself tapping your foot or clapping your hands? What you were doing was feeling the rhythm, and your body was responding to what you heard. Rhythm is a recurring beat that is evenly spaced in time. As an example, feel your own pulse by placing your index and middle fingers on the inside of your wrist on the same side as the thumb. Notice the steady beat.

Can you hear in your mind how "Happy Birthday" sounds when no one is actually singing it? If so, you already know how to audiate (AW di ate): to hear sound mentally without the physical presence of sound. If you can sing a recognizable "Happy Birthday," then you can sing to your baby before birth as well as after. Lullabies or music for relaxing can be a useful choice, especially if your baby does not go to sleep easily. Folk songs could be used as an alternative if parents or caregivers want to hear something different.

I'd like to reassure you that you are extremely likely to be able to hear pitch and rhythm, even if you have never had a music lesson in your life! Nearly always, you will be able to listen and tell the difference in the sounds. I have come across only one child and one adult throughout my entire career in music who could not tell any difference in how pitches sound. On the other hand, I have discovered many adults who are pleasantly surprised to be able to easily distinguish sounds.

HEARING PROTECTION

Before we talk any more about playing music, it is extremely important to be certain that the volume of the music, especially the bass (BASE), is in a safe range in order to protect hearing. If you are planning to go to concerts or any other loud events, use ear muffs to protect the baby's hearing (and ear plugs to protect yours). Absolutely nothing can totally replace the cells that die when any kind of sudden or sustained noise is too loud.

There is a Resources page on my website that lists some free apps that can measure how loud sounds are. If you'd like to search the App Store or Google Play for yourself, enter "decibel meter app." Keep in mind that the numbers are not linear. A reading of 70 dB is 10 *times* as much as 60 dB, not 10 plus.

♪ MUSICAL ACTIVITY: MOVING TO MUSIC WITH YOUR BABY

One of the most useful musical activities is to safely hold or wear the baby on your chest as you move to music. If it is nap time, swaying back and forth gently can help little ones go to sleep. Most babies respond well to rocking, which provides the same rhythmic motion.

If you prefer moving, dancing, or working out to music, all of these activities provide more opportunities to experience rhythm. Our daughter went swing dancing or contra dancing at least every week during her last pregnancy. When her baby was old enough to play, he flapped his arms in a steady beat as he turned his toys into child-safe percussion instruments. In just a few more weeks, he flapped his hands and kicked his feet in rhythm with the music!

If you and your child would like to enjoy moving to this energetic music, go to the first group on the playlist for Chapter 2 on my website, DrJaneJBader.com/chapter-videos. Sometimes, videos are removed on YouTube, so if you find that one is missing, please send an email to me at Jane@DrJaneJBader.com with the subject line "Missing Video." It would be great if you could include the title and chapter number of the missing video. I would really appreciate your help!

MUSIC IN THE BACKGROUND

In order to allow children to absorb experiences of sound, play a variety of music in the background. You could select certain songs for different activities, such as nap time, bath time, and bedtime. While you are listening, think about the mood of the piece and how it could be used to express one's feelings.

It is not necessary to purchase expensive videos to obtain the benefit of music. Streaming services are available, such as Pandora and Spotify; YouTube has an enormous number of performances, as well. Keep in mind that there is a huge variety of composition styles and instruments used in this curated

Chapter 2 playlist on YouTube. There are even some funny videos to showcase musicians' humor!

If all of you don't like something, go on to the next selection. Perhaps the instruments or sound may be different. Don't give up—keep exploring! Composers write music that can be used for all sorts of activities or simply listened to and enjoyed. This playlist covers centuries of music and is not something to be experienced quickly. In fact, if you listen to one selection a week, it could last for several years. Take your time to become acquainted with musical elements beginning around 1300 CE to the present. Additional information is available on my website and can help you learn how to pronounce composers' names and know when they lived.

Do you know what happens when children are learning to eat new foods? It can take over a dozen times of trying the same food item before they develop a taste for it. Music is similar. If something is not appealing, go on to the next selection; however, try the previous one again under different circumstances, maybe even a year later. You may be surprised to find that the sound of something resonates in a way that it didn't at first. Ask yourself why you like or dislike a selection, and try to word your response as specifically as you can.

I have chosen a wide variety of videos, so approach them as an explorer looking for a possible treasure. The list for background music begins after the first group of the Chapter 2 playlist.

Please go on to the next chapter and beyond while you are still listening to everything on this playlist. This collection is meant to be a point of departure over a period of several years for all of you to discover many different kinds of music.

Each selection is designed to introduce you and your children to many different kinds of music throughout history. If you have tried a piece several times and really don't like it, go on to the next one. If you like it, play it for about a week or so before going on. Feel free to make whatever you like part of your own playlist. As you and your child share this musical journey, I will let you know when something should be learned thoroughly before progressing to the next part of this book.

Here are some activities from this chapter that you can do with your children now:

- Sing to and move with your baby both before birth and after.
- Babble: listen and respond to syllabic patterns with pitch and rhythm.
- Experience rhythmic patterns with child-safe percussion instruments.
- Protect hearing by keeping the volume at a safe level.
- Listen to a variety of music in the background.

In the next chapter, you'll get to discover the downbeat, learn how to make up songs, and learn syllables that correspond to pitches. What—you don't believe you can make up songs? As long as you know the tune of a few children's songs, you definitely can, and I'll show you how in Chapter 3!

Chapter 3

Did you know that infants as little as 2 to 3 days old can be capable of recognizing downbeats? In one study, their brain responses were different when the downbeat did not occur as expected. In another study, newborns were observed to respond differently when sounds went up or down. To read more about these studies, look for Winkler as well as Nazzi in Suggested Reading.

The downbeat is an important cornerstone of music; it provides the structure on which everything is built in layers. Feeling the downbeat is an ongoing activity that can be absorbed at any age; it is not something for preschoolers to check off a list, but rather something that is an integral part of all future musical experiences. Have you ever ridden a roller coaster? You go up, up, up, and then suddenly go down, down, down. This downward motion provides energy for the ride. Likewise, it is the downbeat that propels music forward.

HOW TO FEEL THE DOWNBEAT

It is a privilege to share with you a special song that I composed for our grandchildren. I began playing and singing this song with them when they were infants and added a slight, gentle bounce when they were about 6 to 8 weeks old. It's a useful tool to teach children in preschool and beyond, and I hope that all of you will enjoy it, too.

Choose a time when your baby is alert, has a clean diaper, and has been fed, but not too recently. These suggestions are important because babies learn best when they are calm and not distracted by physical discomfort. Usually, a time during the morning or after a nap works well.

♪ MUSICAL ACTIVITY: DOWNBEAT SONG

Think "*DOWN* and up and" until you feel the steady rhythm. It can help to say "*DOWN*" in a louder voice than the other words or to nod your head slightly. Allow yourself to relax on the downbeat, letting gravity do its work. Now, express the rhythmic feeling in your body while standing by relaxing your knees into a small, gentle bounce on the "*DOWN*." If you lift your shoulders higher gradually through the "and up and," you will be prepared for relaxing on the next "*DOWN*."

If a mirror is available, you can stand in front of it so that the baby can see you. Be sure to hold the baby securely, especially the head. If your child is older, you can look directly into their eyes while you hold them. If you're starting this sequence of learning when they are preschool-aged, they will probably enjoy jumping—just be sure to jump up on the "and" so that you land on the downbeat.

There is a demonstration of how to do this activity with babies in the Chapter 3 playlist on my website, DrJaneJBader.com/chapter-videos. You will likely notice the baby's short attention span!

Sometimes, videos are removed from YouTube, so if you find that one is missing, please send an email to me at Jane@DrJaneJBader.com with the subject line "Missing Video." It would help if you could also include the title and chapter number of the missing video so that I can select an alternative. I would really appreciate it!

Sing the words as in the example, emphasizing the italicized words, which show the downbeat:

> *I* love you,
> *YES*, I do!

Be sure to smile really big, and you will likely be rewarded with a precious smile from your baby. These are special moments to remember! Try to repeat all activities five times a day, five days a week. If both you and your baby like this song, feel free to enjoy it as often as you want and make it part of your life.

Congratulations—you have just introduced your baby to the concept of a downbeat! Why is this important? The downbeat is the strongest part of a rhythmic pattern, and everything else depends on its regular recurrence. It magically turns a bunch of notes into what can be easily recognized as music.

How will you know when a child has developed rhythmic feeling around the downbeat? You will usually see some kind of basic body response—that is, some type of movement that indicates they are expressing what they hear with some part of their body. Often, it will be a slight nod of the head, relaxing of the shoulders, or leaning forward. As long as you keep progressing in the activities and repeating experiences as described, your child will normally keep learning.

In a similar way that a child acquires language skills, musical skills grow over a long time with frequent practice, so I have included the downbeat in most of the activities. Sometimes, it can take years of development for a child to intuitively feel and recognizably express the downbeat, depending on the child's age at the beginning, plus the frequency and length of exposure. This learning process happens as language development does. Just because your toddler can talk doesn't mean they have mastered talking; they will continue to refine that skill through adulthood.

♪ MUSICAL ACTIVITY:
DOWNBEAT WITH UPBEATS

Again, choose a time when your baby is alert and has a clean diaper. Remember that babies learn best when they are calm and not distracted by physical discomfort. Often, a time during the morning or after a nap will work well.

When babies are a few months old, it is time to enjoy this activity, which begins with sitting down. Babies should sit just above your knee like they would if they were riding a horse; they can face either toward you or away from you. Begin by gently bouncing them in a steady rhythm. Be sure that the baby has not just finished eating because you don't want to make a milkshake (followed by a mess).

As in the previous example, think "*DOWN* and up and" until you feel the steady rhythm.

The syllables "and up and" are called upbeats because they lead to the downbeat. It can help to say each downbeat in a louder voice. Allow yourself to relax on the downbeat, letting gravity do its work. Now express the rhythmic feeling in your body by bouncing your knee gently in a steady rhythm. Each line should fit into the "*DOWN* and up and" rhythm. If you lift your shoulders higher gradually through the "and up and," you will be prepared to relax on the next "*DOWN*."

The goal for this song is to feel a steady beat between the downbeats. You can watch a demonstration of how to do this activity next on the Chapter 3 playlist.

RIDE a horsey, ride a horsey,
DOWN to town.
LOOK out, horsey,
DON'T fall down!

Did you feel the downbeats? I usually repeat this and slow down on the last line, finishing by lowering the toddler's head while holding it securely. This is a great time to get some tummy sugar or kisses on the head! Change legs and enjoy again. As a bonus, you get a little exercise, too. Try to repeat this activity five times for five days a week. If both you and the baby like this song, feel free to enjoy it as often as you want and make it part of your life.

♪ MUSICAL ACTIVITY: DOWNBEAT FOR OLDER CHILDREN

If you are beginning this program when children are about 3–5 years old, here is another activity to enjoy with them while feeling the downbeat:

Stand up and say "*DOWN* and up and" until you feel the downbeat, using a louder voice if needed each time you say "*DOWN*." Next, bend your knees on the downbeat and return to the standing position. Be sure that you don't bend your knees in any direction that causes pain.

Here are two little songs for you to enjoy next on the Chapter 3 playlist:

*SUN*ny day,
OUT to play.

*RAIN*y day,
IN to stay.

In this video, you can hear how the middle note can make a sunny day sound brighter and a rainy day darker. Listen to the difference in the sounds. Do you think that the sunny day sounds brighter and the rainy day darker? The goal for these songs is to experience the downbeat in a different setting and to discover that emotions can be expressed with musical sounds. Which of these sounds do you think might express being happy or sad?

HOW TO MAKE UP SONGS

What if I told you that you could already make up songs for your baby? All you have to do is add new words to a tune that you already know. Focus on feeling the downbeat first by saying, "*DOWN* and up and," using a louder voice if needed for "*DOWN.*" Remember that the "*DOWN*" is actually relaxing into gravity, not pushing down. If you lift your shoulders higher gradually through the "and up and," you will be prepared to relax on the next "*DOWN.*"

I have selected some examples that are next on the playlist for Chapter 3. If you know and can sing the tune of these songs, you are already most of the way to making up songs on your own:

- "Are You Sleeping?"
- "Mary Had a Little Lamb"
- "London Bridge"
- "Hot Cross Buns"
- "Twinkle, Twinkle, Little Star"

Here are some examples to get you started. Remember to say the downbeat word or syllable in a louder voice if needed or to nod your head slightly. I'll show you where the downbeats are by using uppercase letters combined with italics:

Sing to the tune of "Mary Had a Little Lamb":
NOW it's time to *GO* to bed,
GO to bed, *GO* to bed.
NOW it's time to *GO* to bed and
CLOSE your little *EYES.*

Sing to the tune of "London Bridge":

NOW it's time to *GO* to sleep,

GO to sleep, *GO* to sleep.

NOW it's time to *GO* to sleep.

CLOSE your *EYES*.

Sing to the tune of "Are You Sleeping?":

THIS is how we *GET* you dressed

*EV*ery day, *EV*ery day.

*EAR*ly in the morning, *LATE* in the evening,

*EV*ery day, *EV*ery day.

Sing to the tune of "Hot Cross Buns":

CLOSE your eyes.

GO to sleep.

CLOSE your eyes and go to sleep.

GO to sleep.

Sing to the tune of "London Bridge":

*GET*ting dressed is *WHAT* we do,

WHAT we do, *WHAT* we do.

*GET*ting dressed is *WHAT* we do

*EV*ery *DAY*.

Sing to the tune of "Mary Had a Little Lamb":

TAKE a bath and *SCRUB*, scrub, scrub,

SCRUB, scrub, scrub, *SCRUB*, scrub, scrub.

TAKE a bath and *SCRUB*, scrub, scrub, and

THEN you will be *CLEAN*.

(Be sure to scrub gently.)

Sing to the tune of "Are You Sleeping?":

PUT your pants on, *PUT* your socks on,

THEN your shoes, *THEN* your shoes.

THEN we add a sweater, *THEN* we add a sweater.

YOU'RE all dressed, *YOU'RE* all dressed!

For a different lullaby, sing to the tune of "Twinkle, Twinkle, Little Star":

*SNUG*gle close and *REST* your head.

IT is time to *GO* to bed.

*SNUG*gle close and *REST* your head.

IT is time to *GO* to bed.

*SNUG*gle close and *REST* your head.

IT is time to *GO* to bed.

Now that you see how to combine words with tunes you already know, here are some first lines to get you started. Feel free to come up with silly words; often, that's just what you need to distract a child long enough to change a diaper (or prevent a meltdown). The important thing is that you get to share music and humor with your child.

- *NOW* it's time to...
- *SOON* it will be *TIME* to...
- *HERE* we go to...
- *THIS* is how we...
- *CLOSE* your eyes...
- *GO* to sleep...

Remember that children have a nearly endless capacity for repetition. You will likely be tired of singing something long before they will. If you have trouble singing a tune, you can follow along with the next group of videos as an alternative.

Do not underestimate the power of repetition in making music. When our grandson was 2, I was drying him off and getting him dressed after a sandy excursion to the beach, followed by a shower. The first day I sang, "*THIS* is the way we *GET* you dressed." The second day I sang, "*THIS* is the way we *GET* you dressed." On the third day, his little face lit up, and he smiled with delight as *he* sang, "*THIS* is the way we *GET* you dressed!"

HOW TO DEAL WITH AN EARWORM

No, this is not a literal worm! Having an earworm means that you have a song stuck in your brain and just can't seem to stop thinking about it. Usually, the tune is catchy but simple, and the solution is simply to replace it with something else. It does not work to try to avoid thinking of it; it only becomes more persistent. Instead, try deliberately thinking of something else, such as a bill to pay, an email to write, or a grocery list to make. If you pay attention to something else, the earworm usually fades away, and you forget about it.

HOW TO RELATE SYLLABLES TO PITCHES: SOLFÈGE

Solfège (SOLE fej) is a method for teaching music that associates syllables with pitches of a scale, which can make it easier for young children to understand how the sounds relate to each other. This method is often used to teach children how to sing pitches. The most memorable song I have heard that showcases this idea is sung by Julie Andrews. Her famous performance of "Do-Re-Mi" from *The Sound of Music* is on the Chapter 3 playlist on YouTube.

The syllables with pronunciations are do (DOE), re (RAY), mi (ME), fa (FAH), sol (SOLE), la (LAH), ti (TEE), and then do (DOE) again. You will see that the fifth tone is "sol," but it is sometimes shortened to "so." When you sing the patterns one after another, "sol la" can sound like "so la." I wanted to explain this so that you would not be confused because you might encounter both "sol" and "so" in early childhood music. The next video on the Chapter 3 playlist describes solfège, demonstrates the scale with a name for each syllable, and gives a short introduction.

After you can name the pitches, there are hand signs to learn that go with each syllable, as demonstrated in the excellent video next on the playlist for Chapter 3. Using the hands to make motions that correspond to each syllable you sing is an example of the multisensory approach to learning—using more than one sense to explore and understand a concept.

The next video on the Chapter 3 playlist includes the hand signs with solfège syllables and explains ways to remember them. After that part, you get to sing a song along with them.

Another short video demonstrates the hand signs that go with each syllable and encourages you to sing along as you learn. You will have an opportunity to sing independently, and you can repeat as many times as you like.

Solfège is used for relating pitches to each other and does not include rhythm. To make it easier, I have marked the downbeats for you using uppercase and italic letters in the examples listed. Remember to relax and feel the downbeat first while saying the downbeat in a louder voice if needed or nodding your head slightly. If you lift your shoulders gradually on the upbeats, you will be ready to relax on the downbeat: "*DOWN* and up and." Next on the Chapter 3 playlist are some songs that you probably already know, in which the words have been replaced with the pitch name. After singing these songs with the solfège syllables, you can add the hand signs while you sing the syllables.

"Hot Cross Buns":

MI re do, *MI* re do.
DO do do do re re re re,
MI re do.

"Mary Had a Little Lamb":

MI re do re *MI* mi mi,
RE re re, *MI* sol sol.
MI re do re *MI* mi mi mi
RE re mi re *DO*.

"Merrily We Roll Along":

MI re do re *MI* mi mi,
RE re re, *MI* sol sol.
MI re do re *MI* mi mi,
RE re mi re *DO*.

"Jesus Loves Me":

>*SOL* mi mi re *MI* sol sol,
>
>*LA* la do la *LA* sol sol.
>
>*SOL* mi mi re *MI* sol sol,
>
>*LA* la sol do *MI* re do.
>
>*SOL* mi sol *LA* do,
>
>*SOL* mi do *MI* re,
>
>*SOL* mi sol *LA* do, la
>
>*SOL* do mi re *DO*.

"Rain, Rain Go Away":

>*SOL* mi, *SOL* sol mi,
>
>*SOL* sol mi la *SOL* sol mi.
>
>*FA* re *FA* fa re.
>
>*SOL* fa mi re *MI* do do.

"Jolly Old St. Nicholas":

>*MI* mi mi mi *RE* re re,
>
>*DO* do do do *MI*.
>
>*LA* la la la *SOL* sol do
>
>*RE* do re mi *RE*.
>
>*MI* mi mi mi *RE* re re,
>
>*DO* do do do *MI*.
>
>*LA* la la la *SOL* sol do.
>
>*RE* do re mi *DO*.

ABSOLUTE PITCH

Absolute pitch refers to the ability to name or sing a pitch without a reference sound; it is also known as perfect pitch. On the other hand, relative pitch describes the process of having a reference pitch played and then using the musical distance to identify the sound. There are advantages and disadvantages of having absolute pitch, but relative pitch is a necessary skill for musicians to function.

There is ongoing research regarding the acquisition of absolute pitch, the ages suitable for teaching it, and the mechanisms by which the brain carries out this function. Some researchers believe that infants are born with this capability and lose it as they acquire language. To learn more, look up Saffran and Griepentrog as well as Deutsch in Suggested Reading.

There are online sources that describe how babies and toddlers might be taught absolute pitch. If you're feeling adventurous, search "teach babies perfect pitch" or "teach toddlers perfect pitch." Most people agree that beginning at a young age is more likely to be successful than waiting until elementary school. This book can help you create learning experiences that provide a foundation for future listening skills, and solfège syllables are part of that journey.

Remember to regularly review activities in the previous chapters—especially the downbeat. Here are some things that you can do now with your child:

- Feel the downbeat using a louder voice if needed for the strongest beat.
- Make up songs to sing to your child.

- Sing solfège syllables to your child.
- Make hand signs with solfège syllables.
- Combine solfège syllables with the downbeat in the examples.

When all of you can sing the syllables comfortably, it will be time to explore more music in the next chapter. Toddlers may need years before they can sing on pitch, but they are usually able to say or begin to hum the syllables in rhythm. Are you ready to continue on a wonderful adventure with me and discover the keyboard? Let's explore this instrument together in the next chapter!

Chapter 4

I was thrilled when I got a toy grand piano for Christmas when I was 2 years old. If you don't already have a piano or keyboard, your family will need to borrow, rent, purchase, or request one as a gift. It does not have to be expensive—and, as a bonus, most keyboards include a variety of sounds from different instruments that children like to hear. Even if you have never played a piano or keyboard in your life, I can show you how to have fun exploring it. A word of caution: be sure that children don't drool or spit up (or worse) into the keys!

Our daughter, as well as our grandchildren, were all introduced to the piano before they could sit up. They played all of the notes at both ends of the piano and in the middle. The goal is for your baby to be comfortable exploring both black and white keys.

HOW TO SELECT, USE, AND TAKE CARE OF A KEYBOARD

Begin by searching for a portable electronic keyboard. Be sure it has a built-in speaker, unless you prefer to set up your own sound system. It should include different sounds of instruments, unless you already have a piano, because children are usually attracted to a variety of sounds. Be sure that the default volume is at a safe level in order to protect hearing. If there are stores in your area, visit them to try out different keyboards.

Count the groups of two and three black key groups. You will need at least three groups of two and three black keys. Be sure that the power source of the keyboard is compatible with what is available or what you are willing to spend, such as for batteries.

Next, you will need to decide how you want to use the keyboard:
- Will it always be out and ready for discovery?
- Is the keyboard certified as safe for young children?
- Is it to be used only with adult supervision?

Any buttons that can come off should never be accessible to young children away from observation by attentive adults. Be sure to observe all usual safety precautions for young children.

It is not necessary to buy a stand, seat, or any other accessories at this time. In fact, it will be safer not to have something that could fall or be pulled over. Be sure to treat your keyboard gently. Keep it from falling, being stepped or jumped on, and from having anything put into it, like toys, paper clips, drinks, snacks, or any other object, liquid, or semisolid.

HOW TO FIND A COMFORTABLE HAND POSITION

One of the first questions parents and caregivers ask is how to hold their hands to play a keyboard. The answer is actually relaxed: stand up with your arms at your sides, and your hands relaxed. Keeping the same hand position, lift your hand or hands to the keyboard with your fingers resting lightly on the keys. Are you comfortable? Look at the pictures to see what to do and what not to do.

Correct hand position

Incorrect hand position
Look at the straightened end joint: DO NOT do this.

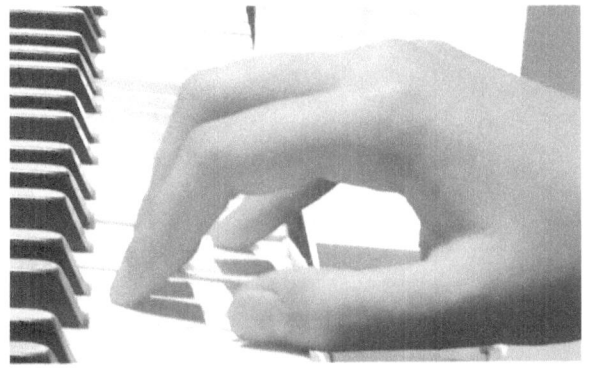

Incorrect hand position
Look at the overly curved fingers: DO NOT do this.

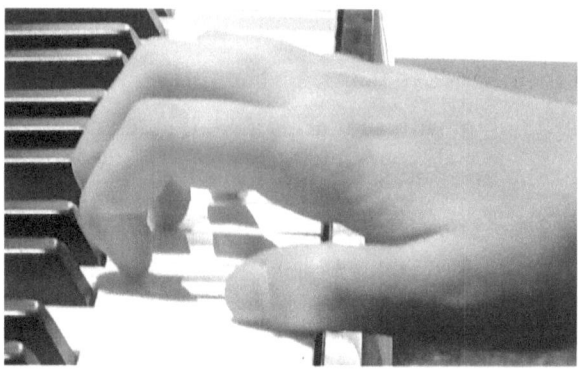

Children generally develop fine motor coordination of the fingers around 4–6 years old. Before that capability, there is an alternative hand position using a gently curved index finger supported by a slightly bent thumb. The tip of the thumb rests just below the bend of the end joint. It can help to think of taking sound out of the keys rather than putting sound into the keys. Notice the supported end joint in this example:

Correct hand position for children

INTRODUCTION TO BLACK KEY GROUPS

Now that you have your keyboard, look at the groups of black keys on the keyboard and count how many there are in each group. You can see that the groups alternate with two and three black keys. Play each key within the group separately, then together. You may use your dominant hand or the other as you like.

Did you know that if you play creative music only on the black keys, it is impossible to play a wrong note? That's because the black keys are all part of a pattern of pitches called the pentatonic (PEN ta ton ic) scale because it has five tones.

♪ MUSICAL ACTIVITY: HOW TO PLAY BY EAR USING PENTATONIC SONGS

This is the perfect time for parents who have not had any formal training in music to learn how to sing and play some pentatonic songs, which are listed in the Chapter 4 playlist on my website, DrJaneJBader.com/chapter-videos.

Sometimes, videos are removed from YouTube, so if you find that one is missing, please send an email to me at Jane@DrJaneJBader.com with the subject line "Missing Video." It will help if you also include the title and chapter number of the missing video so that I can select an alternative. I would really appreciate it!

I have provided the beginning and ending notes for each song to make it easier for you to play on the keyboard. Once you know how the tune goes, you can figure out which notes to play to make the same sound.

Try to spend a little time five days a week on this process until all of you are familiar with these songs and can sing them. Short segments—about 5 minutes long—are ideal; repeat often until you can play them steadily from beginning to end without stopping and starting again. You may need to slow down a little, especially at first.

Please do not rush this process; it is something that children can listen to and learn from. Nearly all the time, parents and caregivers are surprised to discover how well they can play some of these songs. As long as children see you enjoying exploring the keyboard, they will likely want to try, too. Children's songs provide a wonderful foundation of sound experiences that can be useful for generations to come.

When learning music, repetition is an important part of developing a new skill. It usually takes at least five times to practice the same thing correctly in order to succeed. Children will have different abilities to learn, and they will change constantly during growth and development. Please remember that children normally tolerate repetition much better than adults!

I have selected these videos to provide the tune and words for each song. Choose several of these songs to explore on the black keys:

"Hot Cross Buns"
- Start on the right note of the group with three black keys.
- End on the left note of the group with three black keys.

"Mary Had a Little Lamb"
- Start on the right note of the group with three black keys.
- End on the left note of the group with three black keys.
- One verse will be fine, but you're welcome to sing all of them!

"Merrily We Roll Along"
- Start on the right note of the group with three black keys.
- End on the left note of the group with three black keys.

"Amazing Grace"
- Start on the left note of the group with two black keys.
- End on the left note of the group with three black keys.

"Jesus Loves Me"
- Start on the left note of the group with two black keys.
- End on the left note of the group with three black keys.

"Old MacDonald Had a Farm"

Start on the left note of the group with three black keys.

End on the left note of the group with three black keys.

"I've Got Peace Like a River"
- Start on the left note of the group with two black keys.
- End on the left note of the group with three black keys.

"Ten in the Bed"
- Start on the left note of the group with two black keys.
- End on the left note of the group with three black keys.

"Five Hundred Miles" (Chorus)
- Start on the left note of the group with three black keys.
- End on the left note of the group with three black keys.

"Jolly Old St. Nicholas"
- Start on the right note of the group with three black keys.
- End on the left note of the group with three black keys.

Congratulations—you are doing what musicians refer to as "playing by ear!" No, not literally. "Playing by ear" simply means that you are playing by sounds that you hear rather than notes that you read. This is an important part of developing a vocabulary of sounds that all of you can use now as well as in the future.

Children need to learn the meanings of words when learning language, so they can understand what they are hearing and reading. When you discover how to play the part of the song that you sing, you hear how the sounds relate to each other. You probably already know how to tell when the last note in the song is played or sung because of the feeling of finality that comes when you reach the end.

Later in the book, I will show you some patterns that can make it easier to read music; however, actually reading and playing from written music is beyond what this book teaches. The reason is that there are a number of excellent piano method books available that can be used after all of you have developed the musical skills in this book. When you have finished the preparation contained here, you will have a solid foundation to begin reading music if you want to!

Be sure to review and repeat activities from previous chapters. Here are some things that you can do with your children now:

- Select and obtain a keyboard.
- Practice a relaxed hand position.
- Help children learn to support the end joint of the index finger.
- Discover the five-tone scale that simplifies playing by ear.
- Figure out and enjoy songs played only on the black keys.

Would you like to learn about concepts of music that toddlers can learn and use to create music? The next chapter includes musical activities that our grandchildren absolutely loved, so let's dive in!

Chapter 5

W hat if I told you that children could very likely learn important musical concepts before attending kindergarten? If you'd like to nurture your child's brain development through this learning process, introduce these activities one at a time over several weeks or months. Be sure to review past activities to provide the repetition children need to remember long-term. Although many children are able to learn musical concepts between the ages of 2 and 5 years old, some may learn earlier as well as later. By engaging in these activities, reviewing them, and gradually progressing, you will be able to tell if children need more or less time to understand and apply the concepts. If you want to read more, look up Flowers and Zimmerman in Suggested Reading.

Now that you have progressed to this point, I'd like to explain a little more about the learning process that I teach. The goal is to make learning musical concepts easier through gradual steps that continually build on cumulative knowledge and experience. That's the reason I always encourage you to review previous activities.

MULTISENSORY APPROACH TO LEARNING

Numerous studies have shown that involving more than one sense to experience new material makes learning easier to accomplish. In order to help all of you absorb the material as easily as possible, I will suggest an activity that you can hear, see, and do to experience the concept. Educators refer to this type of presentation as multisensory because it involves more than one of the senses. The sense of smell or taste is more challenging to include in everyday teaching, and in the interest of keeping things simple, I will leave it to your imagination to utilize these senses. Feel free to use my suggestions as a place to begin to make your own creative experiences, particularly if you have older children. If you'd like to read more about these topics, look up Condello, Houser, and Marzano and Arredondo, as well as Robinson and Crawford in Suggested Reading.

EXPLORE ONLY ONE NEW IDEA AT A TIME

Be sure to introduce children to only one new idea at a time. Despite many who claim to have the ability to multitask, the human brain can truly focus on only one thing at a time. The illusion of multitasking can be maintained through rapid switching, but the most efficient and effective connections in the brain occur when we focus on a single skill. These activities are designed to make it easier to learn through repetition so that concepts are absorbed as naturally as children learn their native language. If you'd like to read more about these topics, look up Gamble and Grutzmacher in Suggested Reading.

PITCH: HIGH AND LOW

The first concept is pitch, specifically the difference between low and high pitch. This is important because every tune has sounds that go higher and lower in the melody (MEL uh dee), which is the part of a song that you sing.

♪ MUSICAL ACTIVITY: HIGH AND LOW PITCH

Play some keys near the left end of the keyboard as you say "low" in a low voice. Next, play some keys near the right end of the keyboard as you say "high" in a high voice. Encourage your toddler to play low and high sounds on the keyboard. When you are sure that your toddler can recognize low and high sounds, you can add sounds in the middle of the keyboard. Be sure to use a middle voice to describe the middle sounds.

There is an example of low, high, and middle notes on the Chapter 5 playlist on my website, DrJaneJBader.com/chapter-videos. The toddler in this example had just learned to say "middle" and to play middle sounds; he was eager to demonstrate his new skill!

Sometimes, videos are removed from YouTube, so if you find that one is missing, please send an email to me at Jane@DrJaneJBader.com with the subject line "Missing Video." It would help if you could also include the title and chapter number of the missing video so that I can select an alternative. I would really appreciate it!

♪ MUSICAL ACTIVITY: LOW, MIDDLE, AND HIGH EXERCISE

For the next part, be sure to do this activity in a safe area where there are no ceiling fans or other potential hazards. You should also be certain that you are physically able to do the movements as described. During your journey through this book, do not perform any activity that might injure anyone, including yourself.

Hold the toddler securely under the arms facing you and squat down only as far as you are comfortable, saying "low" in a low voice. Now, stand up and extend the toddler up and say "high" in a high voice. Repeat as many times as all of you enjoy for five days a week. This activity will take fewer than 5 minutes.

If you are doing the lifting to represent high, the level of the waist could be used to correspond to the middle sounds. There's an example; it's next on the Chapter 5 playlist.

Be alert for opportunities to relate low and high to things in life; for example, the floor is low and the ceiling is high. Look around and listen wherever you go and describe sounds. On a keyboard, the keys on the left are low and on the right are high in pitch.

Listen to the flute and tuba solos next on the Chapter 5 playlist and ask your toddler which sounds are low and which are high. Make a list with your child of people, animals, and things that can produce low or high sounds. Point out the sounds when you encounter them, and ask children to identify the pitch of each sound, whether it is low or high.

Here are some ways that children could show understanding:

- Point to the floor and ceiling when asked which is high or low.
- Say the words appropriately as their vocabulary grows.
- As their muscles and coordination develop, squat down and stand up to show low and high.
- Have the child play low and high sounds on the keyboard.
- Play low and high sounds on the keyboard and ask the child to identify each.
- Include middle sounds after they are introduced.

DYNAMICS: SOFT AND LOUD

The second concept is called dynamics, meaning how soft or loud musical sounds are. There are a number of levels both in between and beyond, but at the beginning, we are going to focus on soft and loud. Again, be certain that loud sounds are only at a safe level. On a keyboard, adjust the volume switch to show both soft and loud sounds.

As you did with low and high sounds, look for chances to reinforce soft and loud. This is a good time to compare inside voices with outside voices. Be sure that the pitch does not change noticeably because you don't want children to confuse soft and loud with low and high. The reason for them to learn these specific differences is to prevent them from thinking of volume as being high instead of loud and confusing it with high pitch.

♪ MUSICAL ACTIVITY:
SOFT AND LOUD DYNAMICS

Play some sounds on the keyboard that are soft and loud; ask the toddler to identify each. Next, ask the toddler to say "soft" softly and "loud" loudly. During the normal course of every-day activities, ask them to describe different sounds they hear, whether they are soft or loud. So far, I have never observed children who have had any difficulty learning this concept.

If you want to know more, there are special musical terms for soft and loud, respectively: piano and forte (FOR tay). Using two index cards and a marker or pencil, write "PIANO" and "FORTE," one term per card. If children can tell the difference between the words, they can say and point to the correct term for soft and loud. You will be collecting more index cards during the rest of the book, so it could be helpful to use an envelope or paper clip to keep them all together. Save them in a special place with easy access, such as a kitchen cabinet or drawer, if there is room.

Here are some ways that children could show understanding:

- Point to items specifically as they make a soft or loud sound.
- Say the words "soft" and "loud" (or "piano" and "forte") appropriately as their vocabulary grows.
- Make levels of soft and loud sounds with their voice.
- Play soft and loud sounds on the keyboard; ask children to point to the correct card if they can recognize the letters.

TEMPO: FAST AND SLOW

The third concept is tempo, which is how fast or slow the music goes. There are additional levels both in between and beyond, but it is good to start with just fast and slow.

♪ MUSICAL ACTIVITY: FAST AND SLOW TEMPO

Standing together, take several small, quick steps forward while saying "fast." Then take several small, slow steps while saying "slow." Toddlers are usually eager to show "fast" but reluctant to demonstrate "slow."

Play some notes quickly on the keyboard. If you don't know how, try this: using only a group of three black keys, press them one at a time quickly, then press them slowly. Say fast and slow, respectively, as you play them.

There are musical terms for degrees of fast and slow, but to begin, we'll start with allegro (ah *LEG* roh), which means quickly, and andante (ahn *DAHN* tay), which refers to a walking pace. Toddlers will usually consider this to be slow. Using two index cards and a marker or pencil, write "ANDANTE" and "ALLEGRO" on them, one term per card. Save them with the other cards you have made.

Here are some ways that children could show understanding:

- Point to someone running for fast and walking for slow.
- Say "fast" and "slow" (or "allegro" and "andante") appropriately as their vocabulary grows.
- Walk quickly and slowly to show the difference.
- Demonstrate fast and slow on the keyboard and ask children to describe the tempo.

- Play slow and fast sounds on the keyboard; ask children to point to the correct card if they can recognize the letters.

If your toddler is anything like mine was, slow is something they never do!

ARTICULATION: CONNECTED AND SEPARATE

Articulation is another musical concept that children can usually hear easily. When notes are played one after the other, the sound between notes will be either connected or separate. For example, say "Good morning" and observe that the sound is connected. Next, say the same phrase and breathe after each syllable: "Good (breathe) mor-(breathe)ning." Listen for the silence between the separate sounds.

♪ MUSICAL ACTIVITY: CONNECTED AND SEPARATE ARTICULATION

Similarly, musical sounds can be connected or separated. To demonstrate articulation, play two notes one after the other using two fingers. Before you let up the first note, press the second one down, so that the sound is connected before you let up the first note. Next, play the same notes with only one finger and listen for the silence between the notes. Thinking of these sounds as either connected or separate is an excellent example of using words you already know to learn about music, as recommended by Rodriguez, Hair, and Flowers in Suggested Reading.

If you want to know more, the musical term for connected is legato (luh *GAH* toh) and for separated is staccato (stuh *KAH* toh). Using two index cards and a marker or pencil, write

"LEGATO" and "STACCATO" on them, one term per card. Save them with the other cards you have made.

Here are some ways that children could show understanding:

- Walk to show connected sounds, and jump with both feet to show separate ones.
- Say "connected" and "separate" (or "legato" and "staccato") appropriately as their vocabulary grows.
- Identify sounds as connected or separated between notes you play on the keyboard.
- Play connected and separate sounds on the keyboard; ask children to point to the correct card if they can recognize the letters.

TIMBRE

Timbre (*TAM* ber) is a special property of sound that tells you which instrument is being played, even if the same note is played. For example, you can probably tell the difference when the same note is played on a piano, guitar, or trumpet. Many toddlers and preschool children can, too. This is a wonderful time to begin discovering how each instrument sounds so that children can develop their musical preferences. There are some videos after the tuba solo on the Chapter 5 playlist to help you explore unique sounds.

You will know that children understand timbre when they can identify an instrument by its sound. Learning the special sound of each instrument is not essential to go on to the next chapter, but being able to recognize them adds to your and your child's listening experiences. Becoming acquainted with these distinct sounds can be done gradually. If you make notes of which instruments your child likes and which ones they don't, you can compare them in the next chapter to see if their preferences have changed.

In order for children to be ready to go on, it is necessary for them to understand the differences between high and low pitch, soft and loud dynamics, slow and fast tempo, and connected and separate articulation. Even if children have absorbed these concepts easily, please review them to make certain that they are remembered. You will get to use them in the next section.

Children have an amazing capacity for repetition. You don't have to have completely new material every day. You just need to be willing to enjoy a few minutes of playtime with them while they learn. Even if you have studied music before, here are some original ways to make music with children. Our grandchildren absolutely loved creating a thunderstorm on the piano!

CREATIVE SOUND EXPERIENCES ON THE KEYBOARD

♪ MUSICAL ACTIVITY: THUNDERSTORM CREATION

You can see a demonstration of how to do this activity by watching "Thunderstorm" on the Chapter 5 playlist. Be sure to record this unique musical production!

There are three parts:

- The lowest sounds are thunder.
- The middle sounds are rain.
- The high sounds are lightning.

All notes can be used. Be sure that the loudest sounds are at a safe level for everyone.

- Begin with the low rumble of thunder. Gradually become louder.

- Add rain, then more rain until you have a downpour.

- Next, accent with lightning, sudden loud sounds that can be separated if you like.

- Really enjoy the feeling of being safe inside while a storm rages outside.

- Next, allow the lightning and thunder to become softer and the raindrops to become fewer and softer while falling more slowly.

- Finally, the raindrops fade away, and the storm becomes a memory.

This creative expression can be used to show that children have absorbed all four concepts at multiple levels: high and low, fast and slow, soft and loud, and connected and separate.

The next creation can be performed on the keyboard by one to three players using any notes.

♪ MUSICAL ACTIVITY: SPLASHING IN A POOL

Use your imagination to figure out all of these sounds: which ones would be high or low, soft or loud, fast or slow, or connected or separate?

- How do you think little waves would sound? Now play it.

- How do you splash in the water? Now play it.

- Does your toy float in the water? Play that, too.

- If you are leaving a pool, what does going away sound like?

- If you have to let the water out of the pool, what would that sound like?

Try splashing in a pool again, this time using only the black keys or white keys. Does it sound the same or different? Use the other keys and compare sounds using words you learned in this chapter.

Music can be used to express many different ideas or emotions, energy levels, events, settings, and occasions. Think of graduation with the stately march to the stage, or of a race, a circus, or a game. Use your imagination to create new sound pictures of various subjects: a day in the life of a pet, a visit with grandparents, a local outing, a longer trip, the arrival of a new sibling, and many more. Be sure to record these unique performances, too!

♪ MUSICAL ACTIVITY: LARGE MUSCLE MOVEMENT AND EXPRESSIVENESS

If it is time for all of you to have physical activity, try listening to some music by Scott Joplin and John Philip Sousa (SOO suh) on the Chapter 5 playlist. It is nearly impossible to sit still during their music. In fact, one mother shared that her daughter, who was one of my piano students, was joined by the neighborhood kids as they marched around outside with her to their music. This kind of activity can be a lot of fun for everyone. You could add some creativity for older children by letting them choreograph steps, kicks, and arm and hand motions. Now is also a good time to reinforce the downbeat by using a louder voice if needed—"*DOWN* and up and"—along with the music. One creative grandmother turned this activity into a dance party, which was received by the children with great enthusiasm!

How do you recognize the downbeat in these pieces? It is the strongest beat you will hear. Often, pieces will begin on the downbeat; however, others begin before the downbeat. For the Joplin and Sousa selections on the Chapter 5 playlist, there is information on my website about whether each piece begins with a downbeat. Try to figure it out first; afterward, check to see if you identified it accurately.

There is a special name for the note or notes played on the upbeat before you get to the first downbeat: pickup notes, which always lead to the downbeat. For example, "The Bear Went Over the Mountain" and "The Wheels on the Bus" do not begin on the downbeat, but if you feel the rhythm when you say the titles aloud, you can readily find the downbeat. This is an example in which you already know something about rhythmic feeling simply from speaking and listening to your native language. Up to this point, we have talked about how you can learn to feel the stronger downbeat by saying the syllable more loudly; however, there will likely come a time when you simply feel and express the downbeat without actually making it louder.

When children show understanding as described in the musical activities, you will be ready to go to the next chapter. Remember to review activities from previous chapters.

Here are some things for you to do now with your children:
- Identify high and low pitch, soft and loud dynamics, fast and slow tempo, and connected and separate articulation with musical terms.
- Begin learning to recognize the timbre of different instruments.

- Create and record a musical thunderstorm and splashing in a pool.
- Listen and allow your body to feel and respond to the downbeat.
- Experience the downbeat and steady rhythm through large muscle movements.

Would you like to find out more about how music study can open the door to unexpected opportunities, such as college scholarships? In the next chapter, we're going to talk about the development of musical preferences and how musical experience can even assist in getting a job in the future. Ready to begin?

Chapter 6

Preschool is an important time to encourage musical development through listening to a variety of music, as well as through attending recitals and concerts, including virtually. Most musical preferences are formed during this time. As I emphasized previously, be sure that the volume is at a safe level; if not, plan to carry and use ear protection.

DEVELOPMENT OF MUSICAL PREFERENCES THROUGH PERFORMANCE ATTENDANCE

When our daughter was 2 years old, we began attending numerous free concerts and recitals. What's the difference? A piano recital is usually one instrument alone; however, a clarinet, trumpet, or violin recital often includes piano accompaniment. A concert is typically a combination of instruments of different kinds, such as brass, woodwinds, strings, and percussion, although the term can be applied to any musical performance.

There are a number of ways other than online to attend performances of live music without breaking the budget. If you live near a college or university where music courses are taught, there will usually be some kinds of performances that are free. Check their websites, especially toward the end of each semester, to see what you might be interested in hearing. If you are in a rural area, check with the local high school or middle school band, orchestra, or chorus teachers, as well as with church musicians. Many times, there will not be a charge for children under 6. The goal of attending a concert at this age is for each child to find out what kind of music and which instruments they like—as well as what they do not like—while they learn how to be a supportive and appreciative member of the audience.

Some of the best resources for experiencing extraordinary performances are piano festivals and competitions all over the world. I have had the pleasure of attending the Southeastern Piano Festival a number of times. Most are annual events, and some feature young musicians in addition to internationally known performers. There are some links on my website, DrJaneJBader.com/Resources. If you want to find a local event, search for "piano festival" and "piano competition" to find links to truly outstanding performances that can provide enjoyment and inspiration for both children and adults.

For a totally free performance, ask if all of you could attend the dress rehearsal. You could explain that you are trying to help your children learn how to be part of a supportive audience. Assure the people in charge that you will make a quick exit if the children make noise or do not sit reasonably still. This process works for any kind of production: school, community, church, and similar groups.

The dress rehearsal may not be as polished as the final performance, but we found that it was very enjoyable, particularly because we didn't have to dress up or compete (or pay) for parking. For young children who may not be able to sit still and be quiet for a long time, this is a wonderful opportunity to learn about the purpose of an audience and how to support the performers. Sometimes, leaving at intermission may be a better fit for the attention span of young children. Just be sure to sit near an exit in case you need to leave quickly.

CONCERT EXPECTATIONS

Knowing about concert expectations in advance can help everyone to be more comfortable. During a concert featuring acoustic instruments, audience members are expected to sit reasonably still and be quiet with little or no whispering, so that everyone will be able to hear the music easily. Attire can range from jeans and T-shirts to formal. Although many people may dress up a little or a lot, it is not usually a requirement. I strongly recommend bringing stuffed toys and quiet activities to keep little hands busy. I had a bag of activities that I took with our daughter, and it could last up to 2 hours. Be sure that toys do not make noise when (not if) they are dropped!

We had a family rule that a bathroom stop was essential before a timed event. If you need to take children to the bathroom during the performance, slip quietly out while holding a hand for safety. If re-entry is permitted, you should wait until there is a pause or when you hear applause. Some venues do not allow entering again until the entire piece has been performed, so check in advance before purchasing tickets. During intermission, after another bathroom stop, I always provided a safe physical activity for our daughter so that she would be more inclined to sit still and be quiet when the performance resumed. Walking up and down stairs or jumping usually worked well.

If you're hearing a piece with more than one section, which is called a movement, audiences usually wait to applaud until the entire piece is finished; however, I have attended a concert in which the soloist received a well-deserved standing ovation after the first movement! Unless you absolutely know when a piece is finished, a good practice is to wait to applaud until other audience members begin and to stop when everyone else does. Applause is one way to show your appreciation for the musicians' hard work. They can spend many hours of practice for a 3-minute performance—and that doesn't count learning to play the instrument!

There can be reasons for having policies about specific activities that might be limited during performances, particularly concerning safety. Think about the musicians on the stage. Although they practice and rehearse knowing that unexpected events can occur, it is easy to get distracted and lose their place in the music if there is a sudden commotion in the audience. In addition, having people exit and enter during a performance is often distracting to musicians as well as audience members. Because auditoriums are usually dark during performances, having people go in and out could result in falls and injuries. It is similar to going into a movie theater after the movie has started; it takes a while for your eyes to adjust to the darkness.

Many venues have policies to keep everyone as safe as possible. Just be sure to check in advance and plan accordingly.

If all of this sounds like too much trouble, there are other less formal opportunities to hear live performances. Sometimes orchestra members perform at schools, libraries, or even outside venues. Attending a concert in the park could sometimes include a picnic, too.

The Concert Truck is another opportunity to experience a live piano performance, limited only by locations where a truck can be driven and physically parked. It is a mobile concert hall with lights, sound, and a piano. These musicians partner with local communities to provide access to professional performances in many locations that are available for diverse audiences, particularly for marginalized groups. More information is available on my website under Resources.

INSTRUMENTAL PREFERENCES

I need to share some guidance about preferences for different instruments. Some simply require a longer body type and bigger hands to reach keys, tone holes, strings, and similar physical distances. For example, I wanted to get experience reading alto clef and playing the viola (vee OH la), so I registered for a course. The professor was patient and kind while I learned to control the bow, but my arms were simply too short, and my hands were too small to reach the correct hand positions. Although, technically, I could have gotten a reduced-size viola, I was advised not to because the amount of sound a viola can produce is relatively small. Consequently, the next semester I signed up instead for violin, which is a smaller but stronger instrument. I also had to forego learning to play the trombone due to short arms, but I really did enjoy playing the flute. Mine had an offset "G" key that made it much easier for my short fingers to reach. Looking back, I doubt that I would have been successful with a different model because I wouldn't have been able to reach that particular key easily.

Remember when you began listening to videos to explore timbre in Chapter 5? Now is a good time to replay the videos after the tuba solo in the playlist that introduces children to instruments of the orchestra and band. Compare which ones your child likes as well as dislikes, and see if their preferences have changed or remained the same. Keep in mind that becoming skilled at playing any instrument involves cumulative hours of correct practice along with skilled, guided teaching. The effort is worthwhile, though, because it promotes brain development along with academic, social, physical, and personal development.

When the time comes that children think they want to learn to play a musical instrument, I usually recommend renting instruments first to see if children truly like them and actually will practice. When you are looking long-term, be sure that the price of renting or purchasing an instrument, as well as managing the size, would be doable. For example, a flute is relatively inexpensive and easily portable, while a tuba is more expensive and requires a bigger car to transport. A double bass professor I knew always took his instrument with him when he went shopping for a car!

EARLY CHILDHOOD ACCOMPLISHMENTS

One of our family jokes is that our daughter neglected to read the baby book before she was born because she had a different timetable for many events. Consequently, be careful not to underestimate the accomplishments of early childhood. You can set up a gradual learning process by providing opportunities for children to experience musical concepts as an integral part of normal childhood development.

At age 2, I received a toy grand piano, even though no one in my family played any instrument; however, my mother loved music and sang a lot while in the kitchen. On the little piano, there were different colors at the back of the keys that could be used to identify each key. I learned the songs we sang at Sunday school and church because of repetition, and I figured out how to play many of them. I even devised a system for the colors to represent the keys to be played and had scrap pieces of paper with colored stripes as "sheet music." When I was 4, I ran out of keys while trying to play a song one day. I was so frustrated that I actually remember running through the house and yelling, "I don't have enough keys down this-a-way!"

When I was 6 years old, my parents bought my first full-sized piano. Although it was old and needed refinishing, I was thrilled to have a piano with enough keys! It was easy for me to learn to read music because I already had four years of experience with sounds and figuring out how to play songs. It was decades later that I learned from my research what a valuable experience playing by ear could be, and how this process made reading music so much easier.

Another 2-year-old girl received a drum for her birthday and was totally enthralled by the sounds it could make. Although her parents repeatedly tried to encourage her interest in other instruments, nothing else held her fascination like the drums. Fast-forward about twenty years and lots of practice, and she became a professional jazz percussionist!

CHOICES FOR
A MUSICAL FUTURE

It's hard to think of your baby driving a car or getting a job— but it is not too soon to think of the future because it arrives faster than you can ever imagine. When our daughter was 5 years old, she began studying piano. She had been watching me play since she was born and saw how much I enjoyed it, so she wanted to enjoy it, too. When she was 6, she added violin, practiced regularly, and progressed well. She began playing violin for weddings at age 9 and continued through college. Playing violin turned out to be not only a good part-time job, but also an opportunity for a music scholarship. Even if children do not want to major in music, there are ways to get a music scholarship by qualifying through audition and committing to play or sing in a group.

Because of my experience in management as well as teaching at a university, I have been helping adult students to develop leadership capabilities through a nonprofit organization. Although employers value the ability to do a presentation and to have excellent written and oral communication skills, they are looking for some reliable indication of whether or not someone can work in a group and get along with people. Participation in orchestra, band, or chorus can be useful to document these particularly desirable skills in the future.

It is important to consider children's preferences and not require them to fulfill your dreams, but to help them develop their own unique abilities. Sometimes, children go in different directions from what you would prefer, like the percussionist, but you can help them to choose wisely. To assist you, look up Bahnson as well as Burnett and Evans in Suggested Reading to find some excellent books for planning how to have a happy, fulfilled, and successful life.

Remember to review and repeat activities from previous chapters. Here are some things from this chapter that you can do now with your children:

- Listen to a variety of music to discover preferences.
- Use words that you already know to describe characteristics of music that you like or don't like.
- Attend performances both online and in person as available.
- Practice being part of a supportive audience as available.
- Consider choices for a musical future.

What you are doing now to help your children experience musical concepts as part of normal growth and development could have wonderful, far-reaching consequences. If you would like to continue our musical journey by learning about rhythmic patterns with original music, let's go on to Chapter 7!

𝄆 MUSIC FOR THE DEVELOPING BRAIN

Chapter 7

Did you know that the majority of preschool children can tell the difference between a mechanical and an expressive performance? If you'd like to learn more, go to Kalbfleisch in Suggested Reading. You have already learned about the downbeat, so now you are ready to learn about how rhythmic patterns make it easier to give an expressive performance. Think about attempts of early computers to convert text to speech: each syllable was the same tone and rhythm, monotonous and thoroughly boring. In music, treating every note like a downbeat can produce a similar feeling, even if there are no wrong notes.

MECHANICAL AND EXPRESSIVE PERFORMANCES

The first musical example for this chapter contrasts a mechanical and an expressive performance. Go to the playlist for Chapter 7 on my website, DrJaneJBader.com/chapter-videos. Listen with your children and observe that the notes in one example sound like each note is played individually (mechanical) without any expectation of what comes next. Compare that with the other example in which the notes are played in groups of four, with a downbeat beginning each group (expressive). Remember that downbeats are strong; making them louder is simply a tool to help you feel the rhythmic groups. Which example do you enjoy hearing more? Can you feel the downbeat on one of the examples? If you want to read more, look up Hersch and Rodriguez in Suggested Reading.

Listen carefully and try to recognize the mechanical and expressive performances. Notice how the wrists relax on the downbeat as part of the rhythmic feeling. The first example displayed a mechanical performance in contrast to the second, which was expressive. Can you hear the difference? If so, which one would you like to hear more? Of all the times I have ever demonstrated sounds both with and without patterns of rhythm, there has never been an adult who preferred to hear every note as a downbeat. This is another example of how the human brain is hardwired with the capability of perceiving and understanding music.

Sometimes, videos are removed from YouTube, so if you find that one is missing, please send an email to me at Jane@DrJaneJBader.com with the subject line "Missing Video." It would help if you could also include the title and chapter number of the missing video so that I could select an alternative. I would really appreciate it!

RHYTHMIC PATTERNS USING CAKE RHYTHMS

This system of feeling rhythmic patterns is called Cake Rhythms because cakes are usually welcomed and are often used to celebrate an occasion. Patterns of rhythm are grouped by words instead of by numbers or names, and I have found this method to be effective in both teaching and learning. When all of you have learned these patterns, you will be able to celebrate a big accomplishment!

Remember what we were thinking in order to feel the downbeat? "*DOWN*-and-up-and" is the exact same thing that will help you to begin naming these delicious cakes. As previously, I have used capitals and italics in the text to show the downbeats. Be sure to say the downbeat syllable in a louder voice or to nod your head slightly if you need help to feel the rhythm. The downbeat phrase has the same number of syllables as the name for the first cake, and the first syllable is stronger because it is the downbeat: "*RAIN*bow Sprinkle."

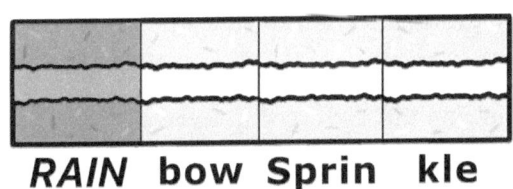

RAIN bow Sprin kle

♪ MUSICAL ACTIVITY: RAINBOW SPRINKLE

Look at this picture of a rainbow sprinkle cake and say in a steady rhythm, "*RAIN*bow Sprinkle, *RAIN*bow Sprinkle, *RAIN*bow Sprinkle, *RAIN*bow Sprinkle." Be sure to feel the downbeats as marked. Next, stand up and take one slow step with each downbeat. You may find it easier to balance by transferring your weight to the other foot just before the next downbeat. If you need an alternative, stand up and stomp one foot on the downbeat. Be sure that you don't take a step for each syllable because we are focusing on large muscle movements only on the downbeat.

When you feel comfortable moving in rhythm with the downbeats, it is time to add the rest of the beats. Clap the same rhythmic pattern with a strong clap for the downbeat as you step, followed by a weaker clap for each syllable. Be sure not to step again until the next downbeat. This is another song that I have written, and this one demonstrates how Cake Rhythms are used. Here are the words to the first verse:

LET'S go make a *CAKE*,
*RAIN*bow Sprinkle *CAKE*.
*RAIN*bow Sprinkle, *RAIN*bow Sprinkle,
LET'S go make a *CAKE*.

Go to the next selection on the Chapter 7 playlist to see "Rainbow Sprinkle Song" so that you can sing along while you step and clap the rhythm. After you can step and clap this rhythm easily, it is time to go to the next one.

You'll probably notice that I introduced you to the biggest pattern of all by asking you to sing along with the example first: *CAKE*. Here is an image for *CAKE*: it is the longest sound and lasts as long as "*RAIN*bow Sprinkle."

CAKE

♪ MUSICAL ACTIVITY: CAKE

Playing and singing music with others includes some way to make sure that everyone begins and ends at the same time. Do you remember what we said while learning about the down-beat? "*DOWN* and up and" worked well then, and it can help you feel the rhythmic patterns here, as well as start at the same time. To get started, say "*DOWN* and up and," then say "*RAIN*-bow Sprinkle" in the same rhythm.

To have some fun with this, ask your child to say "*RAIN*bow Sprinkle" while you say "*CAKE*." The length of "*CAKE*" should be the same as "*RAIN*bow Sprinkle." Now take turns and see if children can make "*CAKE*" last as long as "*RAIN*bow Sprinkle." You could record your saying the cakes at the same time to hear how the rhythm fits together. Practice singing along with the example as you experience the "Rainbow Sprinkle Song."

Be sure that all of you step, sing, and clap with the song five days a week because it provides the foundation to understand how groups of notes are formed from individual notes. These groups form music that you like to hear and enjoy, as you discovered with the example of a mechanical and an expressive performance. Remember to introduce only one new idea at a time to make learning easier for everyone.

When all of you can recognize "*RAIN*bow Sprinkle" along with "*CAKE*" and can step and clap them back together, it is time to learn a new pattern: "*STRAW*berry." The first syllable is stronger because it is the downbeat: "*STRAW*berry."

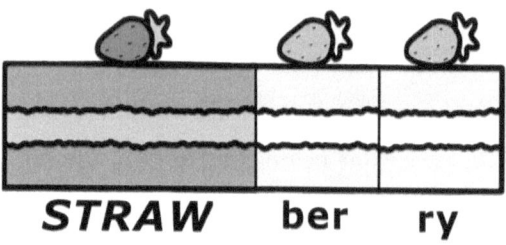

🎵 MUSICAL ACTIVITY: STRAWBERRY

Look at this picture of a strawberry cake and say, "*STRAW*-berry, *STRAW*berry, *STRAW*berry, *STRAW*berry." Be sure to feel the downbeats as marked and make sure that "*STRAW*-" lasts as long as "*RAIN*bow." Next, take one slow step with each downbeat. You may find it easier to balance by transferring your weight to the other foot just before the next downbeat. If you need an alternative, stand up and stomp one foot on the downbeat. Be sure that you don't take a step for each syllable because we are focusing on large muscle movements only on the downbeat.

When you feel comfortable moving in rhythm with the downbeats, it is time to add the rest of the beats. Clap the same rhythmic pattern with a strong clap for the downbeat as you step, followed by a weaker clap for each syllable. Be sure not to step again until the next downbeat. Here are the words for the second verse:

LET'S go make a *CAKE*,

*STRAW*berry *CAKE*.

*STRAW*berry, *STRAW*berry,

LET'S go make a *CAKE*.

Go to the next entry on the Chapter 7 playlist, "Strawberry Cake Song," so that you can sing along while you step and clap the rhythm. Repeat five days a week until "*STRAW*berry" and "*RAIN*bow Sprinkle" are easy to recognize, step, and clap. You could also take turns saying "*STRAW*berry" and "*RAIN*bow Sprinkle," listening to be sure that "*STRAW*" and "*RAIN*bow" as well as "-berry" and "Sprinkle" are said at the same time. Remember to use "*DOWN* and up and" to get started together.

When all of you can recognize "*RAIN*bow Sprinkle," "*CAKE*," and "*STRAW*berry" and can step and clap them back together easily, it is time to learn another new pattern: "*BUT*terscotch." The first syllable is stronger because it is the downbeat: "*BUT*terscotch."

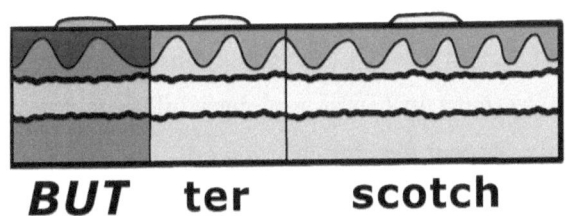

BUT ter **scotch**

♪ MUSICAL ACTIVITY: BUTTERSCOTCH

Look at this picture of a butterscotch cake and say, "*BUT*terscotch, *BUT*terscotch, *BUT*terscotch, *BUT*terscotch." Be sure that you feel the downbeats as marked. "*BUT*ter" should last as long as "*RAIN*bow" and "-scotch" as long as "Sprinkle" in the "*RAIN*bow Sprinkle" example. Next, take one slow step with each downbeat. You may find it easier to balance by transferring your weight to the other foot just before the next downbeat. If you need an alternative, stand up and stomp one foot on the downbeat. Be sure that you don't take a step for each syllable because we are focusing on large muscle movements only on the downbeat.

When you feel comfortable moving in rhythm with the downbeats, it is time to add the rest of the beats. Clap the same rhythmic pattern with a strong clap for the downbeat as you step, followed by a weaker clap for each syllable. Be sure not to step again until the next downbeat. Here are the words for the third verse:

LET'S go make a *CAKE,*
*BUT*terscotch *CAKE.*
*BUT*terscotch, *BUT*terscotch,
LET'S go make a *CAKE.*

The next entry is "Butterscotch Song" on the Chapter 7 playlist so that you can sing along while you step and clap the rhythm. Repeat five days a week until the "*BUT*terscotch," "*STRAW*berry," and "*RAIN*bow Sprinkle" patterns are easy to recognize and clap. All of you could also take turns saying "*BUT*terscotch" and "*RAIN*bow Sprinkle," listening to be sure that "*BUT*ter" and "*RAIN*bow" as well as "-scotch" and "Sprinkle" are said at the same time. Remember to use "*DOWN* and up and" to get started together. If there is another adult, or a child who can talk, each can say the name of one of the cakes together. Remember to make "*CAKE*" as long as each flavor.

When all of you can recognize "*RAIN*bow Sprinkle," "*CAKE*," "*STRAW*berry," and "*BUT*terscotch" and can step and clap them back together, it is time to learn another new pattern: "*AP*ple." The first syllable is stronger because it is the downbeat: "*AP*ple."

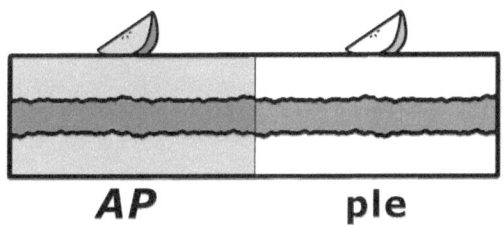

♪ MUSICAL ACTIVITY: APPLE

Look at this picture of an apple cake and say, "*AP*ple, *AP*ple, *AP*ple, *AP*ple." Be sure that you feel the downbeats as marked; "*AP*-" should last as long as "*RAIN*bow" and "-ple" as long as "Sprinkle" in the "*RAIN*bow Sprinkle" example. Next, take one slow step with each downbeat. You may find it easier to balance by transferring your weight to the other foot just before the next downbeat. If you need an alternative, stand up and stomp one foot on the downbeat. Be sure that you don't take a step for each syllable because we are focusing on large muscle movements only on the downbeat.

When you feel comfortable moving in rhythm with the downbeats, it is time to add the rest of the beats. Clap the same rhythmic pattern with a strong clap for the downbeat as you step, followed by a weaker clap for each syllable. Be sure not to step again until the next downbeat. Here are the words for the fourth verse:

LET'S go make a *CAKE,*

*AP*ple *CAKE,*

*AP*ple, *AP*ple.

LET'S go make a *CAKE.*

The next entry is "Apple Song" on the Chapter 7 playlist so that you can sing along while you step and clap the rhythm. Repeat five days a week until the "*AP*ple," "*BUT*terscotch," "*STRAW*berry," and "*RAIN*bow Sprinkle" patterns are easy to recognize and clap. All of you could also take turns saying "*AP*ple" and "*RAIN*bow Sprinkle," listening to be sure that "*AP-*" and "*RAIN*bow" as well as "-ple" and "Sprinkle" are said at the same time. Remember to use "*DOWN* and up and" to get started together. If there is another adult or a child old enough to talk, each can say the name of one of the cakes together in rhythm. You can record yourselves saying your combinations to be sure that *CAKE* lasts as long as each flavor.

♪ MUSICAL ACTIVITY: COMBINING RAINBOW SPRINKLE SEQUENTIALLY WITH OTHER PATTERNS

Clap one of the patterns below and ask children to try to tell what the correct patterns are. You should be able to step, clap, and easily identify all of these flavors of cakes before learning a new pattern.

*RAIN*bow Sprinkle, *CAKE, RAIN*bow Sprinkle, *CAKE*

*STRAW*berry, *CAKE, STRAW*berry, *CAKE*

*BUT*terscotch, *CAKE, BUT*terscotch, *CAKE*

*RAIN*bow Sprinkle, *CAKE, AP*ple, *CAKE*

*RAIN*bow Sprinkle, *AP*ple, *RAIN*bow Sprinkle *CAKE*

*AP*ple, *RAIN*bow Sprinkle, *STRAW*berry *CAKE*

*BUT*terscotch, *STRAW*berry, *AP*ple *CAKE*

*RAIN*bow Sprinkle, *AP*ple, *BUT*terscotch *CAKE*

*STRAW*berry, *BUT*terscotch, APple *CAKE*

Next on the Chapter 7 playlist are some familiar songs that also have rhythms grouped in four beats, like "*RAIN*bow Sprinkle." When it is easy for you to feel the groups of four in each song, you are ready to go on.

♪ MUSICAL ACTIVITY: CHOCOLATE

After all of you can recognize "*RAIN*bow Sprinkle," "*CAKE*," "*STRAW*berry," "*BUT*terscotch," and "*AP*ple" and can step and clap them back together, it is time to learn another new pattern: "*CHOC*olate." The first syllable is stronger because it is the downbeat: "*CHOC*olate." Be sure to say the word in three syllables ("choc-o-late"), not two ("choc-lit").

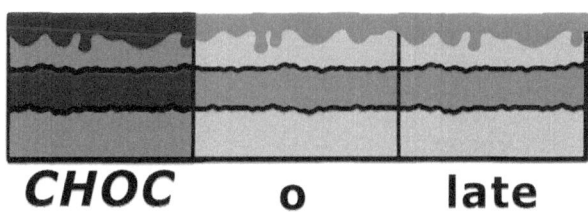

CHOC   o   **late**

Look at this picture of a chocolate cake and say in a steady rhythm, "*CHOC*olate, *CHOC*olate, *CHOC*olate, *CHOC*olate." For this flavor, there are only three syllables, so instead of thinking and feeling "*DOWN* and up and" as you did for "*RAIN*bow Sprinkle," you need to think only "*DOWN* and up." Be sure to feel the downbeats as marked. Next, take one slow step with each downbeat. You may find it easier to balance by transferring your weight to the other foot just before the next downbeat. If you need an alternative, stand up and stomp one foot on the downbeat. Be sure that you don't take a step for each syllable because we are focusing on large muscle movements only on the downbeat.

When you feel comfortable moving in rhythm with the downbeats, it is time to add the rest of the beats. Clap the same rhythmic pattern with a strong clap for the downbeat as you step, followed by a weaker clap for each syllable. Be sure not to step again until the next downbeat. Notice that the rhythm feels different. That's because the number of beats in each group is three instead of four. Here are the words to this verse:

> *LET'S* go *MAKE* a *CAKE*,
> *CHOC*olate, *CHOC*olate *CAKE*.
> *CHOC*olate, *CHOC*olate,
> *CHOC*olate, *CHOC*olate,
> *LET'S* go *MAKE* a *CAKE*.

Go to the Chapter 7 playlist to find "Chocolate Song" so that you can sing along while you step and clap the rhythm. Repeat five days a week until "*CHOC*olate" is easy to recognize and clap in addition to the other cakes. Remember to use "*DOWN* and up and" to get started together.

One difference in this rhythmic pattern is the length of "*CAKE*." The "*CAKE*s" are not interchangeable, so do not try yet to combine anything other than "*CHOC*olate" and "*CAKE*."

There are some more songs on the playlist for Chapter 7 after "Chocolate Cake Song" for you to select from to help you experience the "*CHOC*olate" pattern.

♪ MUSICAL ACTIVITY: IDENTIFYING RAINBOW SPRINKLE AND CHOCOLATE PATTERNS

Listen to or sing the songs with the videos after "The Bear Went Over the Mountain" on the Chapter 7 playlist and decide if "*CHOC*olate" or "*RAIN*bow Sprinkle" rhythmic groups are present. When that is easy, listen to whatever music you like and identify the downbeat.

Here's a tip: when you feel the downbeat, listen to the pattern to see if it goes with "*RAIN*bow Sprinkle" or "*CHOC*olate." All of you are ready to go on if you can identify all of the rhythmic patterns in this chapter and clap them accurately while taking one step on the downbeats.

Remember to review activities from the previous chapters. Here are some things you can do with your children now:

- Recognize the difference between mechanical and expressive performances.
- Explore and learn to recognize the Cake Rhythms:
  - *RAIN*bow Sprinkle
  - *CAKE*
  - *STRAW*berry
  - *BUT*terscotch
  - *AP*ple
  - *CHOC*olate

Now that you know how to keep a steady beat in rhythmic patterns, it is time to be introduced to the names of all the keys.

Remember the songs you have been reviewing that you played in Chapter 4 using only the black keys? If you learned them well, now it is time to revisit some of those tunes, so let's continue our musical journey with the discovery of the white keys!

Chapter 8

By now, you must be wondering about how the keyboard is designed to make music and what the keys are called. I can satisfy your curiosity in this chapter!

INTRODUCTION TO KEYBOARD LAYOUT

Can your child say the alphabet from A to G and recognize the letters? Then it is not too early to become acquainted with the keyboard and how you can learn to make music. The first white key that I would like to introduce to you is between the group of two black keys, and it is called D.

NEIGHBOR GROUP D, C, AND E

♪ MUSICAL ACTIVITY: D

Find each group of two black keys on the keyboard and identify the D white key between them. Play each D; next, play each D while saying "D."

Beginning in the middle of the keyboard, play each D to the left and back to the middle. Listen carefully to hear that the pitch becomes lower, then higher. Beginning in the middle of the keyboard, play each D to the right and back to the middle. Listen carefully to hear that the pitch becomes higher, then lower. Plan to do this activity five days a week.

Finally, draw a large, uppercase D on a 3″ × 5″ index card and have your child trace the letter with an index finger while saying "D." Save the card in a special place with the previous ones. Each key will end up with its own card when we finish. Remember, the side of a kitchen cabinet or inside a drawer can be a convenient place for easy access to materials for learning.

Before going on, all of you need to be able to do the following:

- Look at the D on the index card and say "D."
- Point to all the Ds individually on the keyboard.
- Play all the Ds on the keyboard.

Repeat and review until this activity becomes easy for all of you. After you can identify and play all the Ds easily, it is time to introduce the next-door neighbor to the left, which is C.

♪ MUSICAL ACTIVITY: C

Ask your children what letter comes before D in the alphabet. They can figure it out by singing the first line of the alphabet song. Find each group of two black keys on the keyboard and identify the C white key to the left of D. Play each C; next, play each C while saying "C." The C in the middle has a special name: "Middle C."

Beginning with Middle C, play each C to the left and back to the middle. Listen carefully to hear that the pitch becomes lower, then higher. Beginning again with Middle C, play each C to the right and back to the middle. Listen carefully to hear that the pitch becomes higher, then lower. Plan to do this activity five days a week.

Finally, draw a large, uppercase C on a 3″ × 5″ index card and have your child trace the letter with an index finger while saying "C." Save the card with the others in a special place.

Next, it is time to explore the combination of C and D. Is C higher or lower in pitch than D? Listen carefully to hear that C is lower than D. Play C and D one after the other, then D and C. Next, play C and D together; have you ever heard that sound before? It's the first sound in "Chopsticks." If you play C and D separately, they are the first sounds in "Happy Birthday."

Before going on, all of you need to be able to do the following:

- Look at the C on the index card and say "C."
- Point to all the Cs individually on the keyboard.
- Play all the Cs on the keyboard.
- Hold up a C or D flash card and play the correct note.

After you and your child can identify and play all the Cs and Ds easily, it is time to introduce the next-door neighbor to the right of D, which is E.

♪ MUSICAL ACTIVITY: E

Ask your children what letter comes after D in the alphabet. They can figure it out by singing the first line of the alphabet song. Find each group of two black keys on the keyboard and identify the E white key to the right. Play each E; next, play each E while saying "E."

Beginning in the middle of the keyboard, play each E to the left and back to the middle. Listen carefully to hear that the pitch becomes lower, then higher. Beginning in the middle of the keyboard, play each E to the right and back to the middle. Listen carefully to hear that the pitch becomes higher, then lower. Plan to do this activity five days a week.

Finally, draw a large, uppercase E on a 3″ × 5″ index card and have your child trace the letter with an index finger while saying "E." Save the card in a special place with the others.

Play a C, D, or E, and ask your child to look at and name the note you played. Next, hold up a C, D, or E flash card and ask your child to play the correct note. Repeat and review until this activity is easy for all of you.

Next, it is time to explore the combination of C and E. Play C and E one after the other, then E and C. Is C higher or lower in pitch than E? Listen carefully to hear that C is lower than E. Next, play C and E together. If you play C first and then E, they are the first sounds in "The Bear Went over the Mountain." To review, play a C, D, or E, and ask your child to look at and name the note you played. Next, hold up a C, D, or E flash card and ask them to play the correct note.

♪ MUSICAL ACTIVITY: TRANSPOSITION OF "HOT CROSS BUNS"

Do you remember "Hot Cross Buns" as you played it on the black keys earlier? You can also play it on the CDE group. Start on the E and end on the C. Congratulations—you have just transposed your first song! What does that mean? You played a song in a different position on the keyboard and kept exactly the same tonal pattern.

Before going on, all of you need to be able to do the following:

- Look at the E on the index card and say "E."
- Point to all the Es individually on the keyboard.
- Play all the Es on the keyboard.
- Hold up a C, D, or E flash card and play the correct note.

After you and your child can identify and play all the Cs, Ds, and Es easily, it is time to introduce the next neighbor group of keys: F, G, A, and B.

NEIGHBOR GROUP F, G, A, AND B

♪ MUSICAL ACTIVITY: F

Ask your children what letter comes after E in the alphabet. They can figure it out by singing the first line of the alphabet song. Find each group of three black keys on the keyboard and identify the F white key between the E and the first black key in the group. Play each F; next, play each F while saying "F."

Starting in the middle of the keyboard, play each F to the left and back to the middle. Listen carefully to hear that the pitch becomes lower, then higher. Beginning in the middle, play each F to the right and back to the middle. Listen carefully to hear that the pitch becomes higher, then lower. Plan to do this activity five days a week.

Finally, draw a large, uppercase F on a 3″ × 5″ index card and have your child trace the letter with an index finger while saying "F." Save the card with the others in a special place.

Play a C, D, E, or F, and ask your child to look at and name the note you played. Next, hold up a C, D, E, or F flash card and ask them to play the correct note. Repeat and review until this activity is easy for all of you.

After children do these activities easily, it is time to explore the combination of C and F. Is the C higher or lower in pitch than the F? Listen carefully to hear that C is lower than F. Play C and F one after the other, then F and C. Next, play C and F together. If you play C first and then F, they are the first sounds in "The Wheels on the Bus."

Before going on, all of you need to be able to do the following:
- Look at the F on the index card and say "F."
- Point to all the Fs individually on the keyboard.
- Play all the Fs on the keyboard.
- Hold up a C, D, E, or F flash card and play the correct note.

After children can identify and play all the Cs, Ds, Es, and Fs easily, it is time to introduce the next-door neighbor to the right of F, which is G.

♪ MUSICAL ACTIVITY: G

Ask your children what letter comes after F in the alphabet. They can figure it out by singing the first line of the alphabet song. Find each group of three black keys on the keyboard and identify the G white key between the F and the middle black key in the group. Another way to find it is to look at each group of three black keys; the G white key is between the first and second black keys in the group. Play each G; next, play each G while saying "G."

Starting in the middle of the keyboard, play each G to the left and back to the middle. Listen carefully to hear that the pitch becomes lower, then higher. Beginning in the middle of the keyboard, play each G to the right and back to the middle. Listen carefully to hear that the pitch becomes higher, then lower. Plan to do this activity five days a week.

Finally, draw a large, uppercase G on a 3″ × 5″ index card and have your child trace the letter with an index finger while saying "G." Save the card with the others in a special place.

Before going on, all of you need to be able to do the following:
- Look at the G on the index card and say "G."
- Point to all the Gs individually on the keyboard.
- Play all the Gs on the keyboard.
- Hold up a C, D, E, F, or G flash card and play the correct note.

After children do these activities easily, it is time to explore the combination of C and G. Is the C higher or lower in pitch than the G? Listen carefully to hear that C is lower than G. Play C and G one after the other, then G and C together. If you play C first and then G, they are the first sounds in "Twinkle, Twinkle Little Star." To review, play a C, D, E, F, or G and ask children to look at and name the note you played. Next, hold up a flash card and ask them to play the correct note.

♪ MUSICAL ACTIVITY: TRANSPOSITION OF "MARY HAD A LITTLE LAMB"

Remember when you played "Mary Had a Little Lamb" on the black keys? Now you can play it on the white keys. Place your right hand so that your thumb is on Middle C and your pinky is on G. Your fingers in between should rest lightly on the keys, with one finger on each white key. The first note is E, and the last one is C. Try to make it sound just like you know it sounds. Do you remember transposing "Hot Cross Buns"? Well, you just transposed "Mary Had a Little Lamb"!

After children can identify and play all the Cs, Ds, Es, Fs, and Gs easily, it is time to introduce the next-door neighbor to the right of G, which is A.

♪ MUSICAL ACTIVITY: A

Ask your children what letter is first in the alphabet. They can figure it out by singing the first line of the alphabet song. The keyboard alphabet includes only the letters from A to G, and then it starts over again. In each group of three black keys on the keyboard, the A is between the two black keys on the right, so you can identify the A white key between the G and the right black key in the group. Play each A; next, play each A while saying "A."

Starting in the middle, play each A to the left and back to the middle. Listen carefully to hear that the pitch becomes lower, then higher. Beginning in the middle of the keyboard, play each A to the right and back to the middle. Listen carefully to hear that the pitch becomes higher, then lower. Plan to do this activity five days a week.

Finally, draw a large, uppercase A on a 3″ × 5″ index card and have your child trace the letter with an index finger while saying "A." Save the card with the others in a special place.

Before going on, all of you need to be able to do the following:
- Look at the A on the index card and say "A."
- Point to all the As individually on the keyboard.
- Play all the As on the keyboard.
- Hold up a C, D, E, F, G, and A flash card and play the correct note.

♪ MUSICAL ACTIVITY: B

Ask your children what letter comes after A in the alphabet. They can figure it out by singing the first line of the alphabet song. In each group of three black keys on the keyboard, the B is to the right of the group of three black keys so that you can identify the B white key between A and C. Play each B; next, play each B while saying "B."

Starting in the middle, play each B to the left and back to the middle. Listen carefully to hear that the pitch becomes lower, then higher. Beginning in the middle of the keyboard, play each B to the right and back to the middle. Listen carefully to hear that the pitch becomes higher, then lower. Plan to do this activity five days a week.

Finally, draw a large, uppercase B on a 3″ × 5″ index card and have your child trace the letter with an index finger while saying "B." Save the card with the others in a special place.

Before going on, all of you need to be able to do the following:

- Look at the B on the index card and say B.
- Point to all the Bs individually on the keyboard.
- Play all the Bs on the keyboard.
- Hold up all of the flash cards separately and play the correct note.

Congratulations—you have learned the name and location of each of the white keys on the keyboard! Remember to review activities in the previous chapters as well as this one.

Here are some more fun activities that you can do with your children:

- Identify, in order, the names of each key on the keyboard from left to right, then right to left.
- Sing each key name in the range of notes that you can comfortably reach while you play it.
- Match the card with the key on the keyboard and play it.

In the next chapter, you will learn where to place your hands to play some songs that you already know, so let's get started!

Chapter 9

In this chapter, we're going to explore how to figure out where to place your hands on the keyboard, as well as how to play the songs on the white keys that you have previously been playing on the black keys. Remember to keep a relaxed hand position, as demonstrated below. To review, stand up and let your arms and hands relax by your sides. Keeping that same hand position, sit down and let your hands rest lightly on the keyboard.

Correct hand position

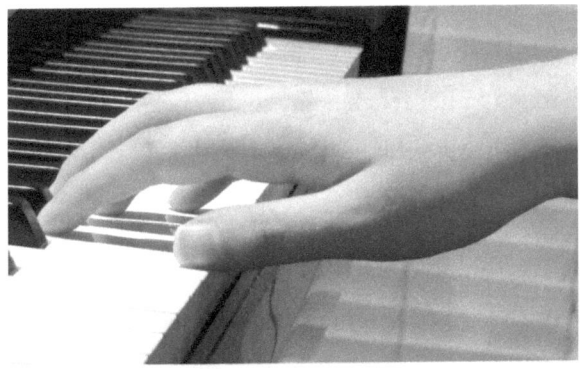

FINGER NUMBERS

If your children can count from one to five, they can learn the finger numbers used for piano and keyboard. Here's a list to help:

1. thumb
2. index finger
3. middle finger
4. ring finger
5. pinky

These numbers are the same for each hand, and it doesn't matter if you're right- or left-handed.

Keep in mind that if children play violin, viola, cello (CHEL oh), or double bass (BASE), the fingering is different. Brass instruments will also have different fingering due to valves, and the trombone doesn't even have fingering—just slide positions. If you are wondering how it could be different, I'll explain. For strings, the left thumb is used to assist in holding the instrument in the proper position, while the four fingers hold the strings down in different positions. As a result, the index finger is the first one that could physically press down on a string. Our daughter played violin from first grade until beyond college, and I listened to her teacher say many times, "The index finger is one because everyone knows a thumb isn't a finger!"

♪ MUSICAL ACTIVITY: FINGER NUMBERS

Because the thumb is used to play notes on the keyboard, we will follow the finger numbers as listed above. Hold your hands in front of you, facing each other, with your fingers slightly apart. You should be looking at your thumbs. Now gently touch your fingertips together one number at a time: 1, 2, 3, 4, and 5. For the next part, mix up the numbers, such as 2, 4, 3, 5, and 1. Try some different combinations until this is easy for you. Children can demonstrate these numbers, too, as soon as their fine motor coordination has developed to this point, usually at around 4–6 years old.

Write on five separate index cards LH 1, LH 2, LH 3, LH 4, and LH 5. You can mix them up in a bag or container. Do the same for the right hand: write on five separate index cards RH 1, RH 2, RH 3, RH 4, and RH 5, and place them in a separate bag or container. Draw one out of the container for the right hand (RH) and left hand (LH). As an example, if you draw LH 2 and RH 4, touch LH (left) 4 to RH (right) 2. Repeat with the rest of the finger numbers. Plan to play this game five days a week. When all of you can play this game accurately and easily, you are ready to learn a hand position.

MIDDLE C POSITION

Do you remember the hand position when you played "Mary Had a Little Lamb" for the first time on the white keys? Your right thumb was on Middle C, and your pinky was on G. Place your right hand in this position with the fingers relaxed and curved slightly. Now add your left hand, beginning with your thumb on Middle C and your pinky on F below Middle C. You should have both thumbs on or close to Middle C, and one finger on each of the other white keys. Here's a picture to show you what it looks like:

Middle C position

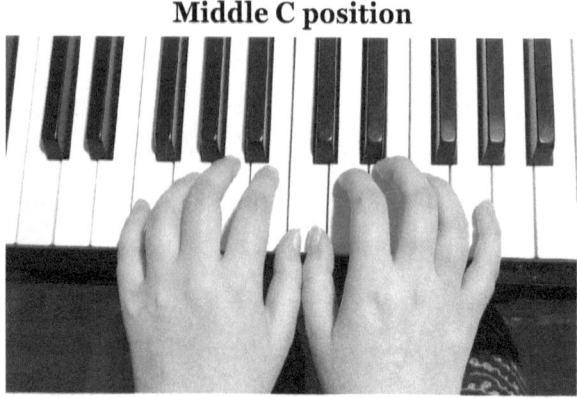

Congratulations—your hands are now in Middle C position! Notice that both thumbs may not fit; if not, then simply place one thumb on Middle C so that it will be ready to play when you need it. In order to become familiar with this hand position, start with your hands in your lap, then return them to Middle C position. Repeat five days a week until you are comfortable placing your hands in this position. The more often you practice getting to this position, the sooner you will be confident about where your hands go.

Next, it's your child's turn if their hands are large enough and they can keep a relaxed hand position. If not, they can play with one supported index finger as shown in the next image.. It is important that the child does not develop bad habits that can interfere with playing a keyboard in the future, such as letting the end joint of the index finger collapse or curling the fingers tightly, as shown in the examples of incorrect hand positions in Chapter 4.

Correct hand position for children

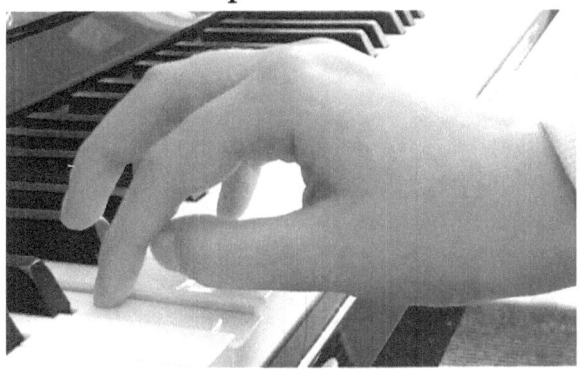

SONGS IN MIDDLE C POSITION

Now that you have learned the first hand position on the white keys, it is time to enjoy some of the songs that you previously played on the black keys. To help you know which hand to start and end with, I'll use RH for right hand and LH for left hand, just as we did while learning finger numbers. If you'd like to listen, go to the playlist for Chapter 9 on my website, DrJane-JBader.com/chapter-videos.

Sometimes, videos are removed from YouTube, so if you find that one is missing, please send an email to me at Jane@DrJaneJBader.com with the subject line "Missing Video." It would be great if you could also include the title and chapter number of the missing video so that I could select an alternative. I would really appreciate your help!

"Hot Cross Buns"
- Start on E (RH 3) and end on C (RH 1 or LH 1).

"Mary Had a Little Lamb"
- Start on E (RH 3) and end on C (RH 1 or LH 1).

"Merrily We Roll Along"

  • Start on E (RH 3) and end on C (RH 1 or LH 1).

"Amazing Grace"

  • Start on G (LH 4) and end on C
    (RH 1 or LH 1).

"Jesus Loves Me

  • Start on D (RH 2) and end on G (LH 4).

"Old MacDonald Had a Farm"

  • Start on C (RH 1 or LH 1) and end on C (RH 1 or LH 1).

"I've Got Peace Like a River"

  • Start on G (LH 4) and end on C (RH 1 or LH 1).

"Ten in the Bed"

  • Start on G (LH 4) and end on C (RH 1 or LH 1).

"Five Hundred Miles" (Chorus)

  • Start on C (RH 1 or LH 1) and end on C (RH 1 or LH 1).

"Jolly Old St. Nicholas"

  • Start on E (RH 3) and end on C (RH 1 or LH 1).

Now that you have become acquainted with the keyboard, it is time to learn how to navigate up and down. Wait a minute—we've talked about right and left with high and low pitch, so where do you get up and down? Here's where: when you look at written music, the notes closer to the top of the page on the staff have a higher pitch than notes closer to the bottom of the page. As a result, keys that go in the direction of the highest pitch are said to go up, while keys that go in the direction of the lowest pitch are said to go down. In short, "up" is toward the right, and "down" is toward the left on the keyboard and piano. I'll be using "up" and "down" to help you become familiar with how those words are commonly used with a keyboard.

TREBLE AND BASS CLEFS

Once you can easily place your hands in Middle C position, I'm going to show you what the note Middle C looks like on written music—after we identify the parts that make up the map of sound. Remember that you have already been introduced to these ideas; you are simply putting a face to a name. To begin, from Middle C up, there is a sign that indicates that part of the keyboard. Here is a picture of a treble (TREB uhl) clef:

Treble clef

From Middle C down, there is a sign that indicates that part of the keyboard. Here is a picture of a bass (BASE) clef:

Bass clef

♪ MUSICAL ACTIVITY: TREBLE AND BASS

Ask your child to name and say "treble" and play some keys on the upper part of the keyboard. Do the same for the lower keyboard for "bass." After your child can repeatedly identify the clefs correctly and the range of notes that correspond, you are ready to go on to the next section.

GRAND STAFF

When the treble or bass clef is written on a staff, it is called a treble or bass staff. When they are combined, they are called the grand staff and are connected by Middle C as shown by both notes, which is how Middle C is represented in each staff:

Grand staff with Middle C

♪ MUSICAL ACTIVITY:
GRAND STAFF WITH MIDDLE C

Show children the image of the grand staff and ask them to find Middle C on the keyboard. Next, ask them to look at and listen to notes you play and tell if they are part of the treble or bass staff. Finally, encourage them to play notes for themselves and tell you if they are treble or bass. As you can see in the example, Middle C can be part of both the treble and bass staves (plural of staff).

SONGS FOR MUSICAL DISTANCES

It is much easier to remember sounds by relating them to songs you have already learned. Adding these songs to your playlist and enjoying them in the car can help you to have more time to build a foundation for learning music. Doing essential house-hold activities together five days a week can also be a great opportunity to sing or listen. These songs make up the rest of the Chapter 9 playlist:

- "Happy Birthday"
- "The Bear Went over the Mountain"
- "The Wheels on the Bus"
- "Twinkle, Twinkle Little Star"

The first two or three sounds in each song are the ones we will focus on because hearing and recognizing these sounds is important before learning to read music. As long as you know the first line of each song, you will be able to compare these sounds with others. It is important that you be able to hear the differences in these sounds before going on.

Remember to review activities from the previous chapters. Here are some things you can do with your children now:

- Play a game of "name the finger numbers."
- Measure how fast you can place your hands in Middle C position from your lap.

- Play songs that you already know on the white keys.
- Identify the treble clef, bass clef, and grand staff.

If you are ready to see how we use these important sounds and learn about musical distances, let's go to Chapter 10!

Chapter 10

In this chapter, we're going to learn about other ways to navigate the keyboard. One of these ways is by hearing (and then seeing) how sounds relate to each other. Intervals are the musical distance between two notes. The easiest way to learn tonal relationships is by comparing sounds with songs that you already know. This process could take days, weeks, or longer. Remember to learn only one interval at a time, and be sure to review what you already know. Plan to spend a little time five days a week on this process until you are familiar with these sounds. Short segments of up to 5 minutes are ideal; repeat often until all of you can name these sounds with confidence.

MELODIC AND HARMONIC INTERVALS

Intervals can be played one after another or together. When they're played one at a time, they are called melodic (muh *LAHD* ic) intervals because the melody is the part of the song that you sing. When intervals are played together, they are called harmonic (hahr *MAHN* ic) because they form harmony, which supports the melody. I play them both ways in the videos to make it easier for you to hear the sounds.

Imagine a flight of stairs and stepping up, then down. Likewise, the first interval we're going to discover is called a step. If you sing "do re do," you will have sung a step. As steps do, musical sounds also go up and down.

♪ MUSICAL ACTIVITY: STEP OR SECOND (2ND)

Relax your right arm and hand by your side. Keeping your hand in the same relaxed position, place your right hand with 1 on C and 5 on G. This will be your basic hand position for learning intervals. This is the same as the right hand position of the Middle C position. Play 1 on C, then 2 on D; reverse the process and play D, then C. Now play C and D together. Does this sound like "Chopsticks"? Listen carefully to hear the sound of each note within the combination. It may be easier to hear if you sing each note. Can you hear how it sounds similar to the first four notes of "Happy Birthday"? Keep listening for just a few minutes each day until you can recognize this sound easily. Listen to a step (also called a "2nd") on the Chapter 10 playlist on my website, DrJaneJBader.com/chapter-videos.

Sometimes, videos are removed from YouTube, so if you find that one is missing, please send an email to me at Jane@DrJaneJBader.com with the subject line "Missing Video." It would help if you could also include the title and chapter number of the missing video so that I can select an alternative. I would really appreciate it!

Take an index card and write "2nd" and "STEP" on it. Let your child trace the number and letters of the word with an index finger. Save the card with the others because you will use it with the next interval.

♪ MUSICAL ACTIVITY: SKIP OR THIRD (3RD)

After all of you are comfortable hearing and identifying a step, it is time to learn the next interval: a skip. Imagine the same flight of stairs—but this time, think of skipping one each time you put your foot down. If you sing "do mi do," you will have sung a skip.

Using the same hand position, play 1 on C, then 3 on E; reverse the process and play E, then C. Now play C and E together. Listen carefully to hear the sound of each note within the combination. It may be easier to hear if you sing each note. Can you hear how it sounds like the first two notes of "The Bear Went over the Mountain"? Keep listening for just a few minutes at a time until you can recognize this sound easily. There is an example of a skip (also called a "3rd") next on the Chapter 10 playlist.

Take an index card and write "3rd" and "SKIP" on it. Let your child trace the number and letters of the word with an index finger. Save the card with the one labeled "STEP" and "2nd". You will use them in the next activity.

♪ MUSICAL ACTIVITY: STEPS AND SKIPS

Play a step or skip and ask your child to point to the correct card. If someone else is available, close your eyes and have them play steps and skips for you and your child to identify. As an alternative, listen to the videos instead. Review until all of you identify both intervals accurately. For steps, you can play not only C and D, but also D and E, F and G, G and A, and A and B. For skips, you can play F and A, G and B, and C and E.

Plan to review for a few minutes five days a week until all of you can identify these sounds with confidence. Compare the beginning sounds of "Happy Birthday" and "The Bear Went over the Mountain." It may be easier for children to remember the name of the song instead of the name of the interval. As long as they can identify the song and recognize the sound that goes with it, that's fine.

After all of you are comfortable recognizing steps and skips, ask your child what number comes after 3. If they say 4, that's right—and the next interval is a fourth, shown as "4th." If you sing "do fa do," you will have sung a 4th. One song that begins with a 4th is "The Wheels on the Bus."

♪ MUSICAL ACTIVITY: FOURTH (4TH)

Using the same hand position, play 1 on C, then 4 on F; reverse the process and play F, then C. Now play both C and F together. Listen carefully to hear the sound of each note within the combination. It may be easier to hear if you sing each note. Can you hear how it sounds like the first two notes of "The Wheels on the Bus"? Keep listening for just a few minutes five days a week until you can recognize this sound easily. There is an example of a "4th" next on the Chapter 10 playlist.

Take an index card and write "4th" on it. Let your child trace the number with an index finger. Save the card with the others because you will use them for the next activity.

♪ MUSICAL ACTIVITY: STEPS, SKIPS, AND FOURTHS (4THs)

Play a step, skip, or 4th and ask your child to point to the correct card. If someone else is available, close your eyes and have them play 2nds, 3rds, and 4ths on the keyboard for you and your child to identify. As an alternative, listen to the videos instead and ask children to point to the card that identifies each. Be sure that you know how to recognize all of these intervals before going on.

Tip: when you are trying to figure out what the interval is, sometimes it can help to eliminate what it is not. Sing the first notes of "Happy Birthday." Does it fit? If not, sing the first notes of "The Bear Went over the Mountain." Does it fit? If not, sing the first notes of "The Wheels on the Bus."

Try to review for a few minutes five days a week until all of you can identify these sounds with confidence. There are a number of ways for you to play 4ths: C and F, D and G, E and A, G and C, A and D, and B and E.

After all of you are comfortable recognizing steps, skips, and 4ths, ask your child what number comes after 4. If they say 5, that's right—and the next interval is a fifth, shown as "5th". If you sing "do sol do," you will have sung a 5th. One song that begins with a 5th is "Twinkle, Twinkle, Little Star."

♪ MUSICAL ACTIVITY: FIFTH (5TH)

Using the same hand position, play 1 on C, then 5 on G; reverse the process and play G, then C. Now play both C and G together. Listen carefully to hear the sound of each note within the combination. It may be easier to hear if you sing each note.

Can you hear how it sounds like the first four notes of "Twinkle, Twinkle, Little Star"? Keep listening until you can hear this sound. There is an example of a "5th" next on the Chapter 10 playlist.

Take an index card and write "5th" on it. Let your child trace the number with an index finger. Save the card with the others to use in the next activity.

♪ MUSICAL ACTIVITY:
STEPS, SKIPS, 4THs, AND 5THs

Play a step, skip, 4th, or 5th, and ask your child to point to the correct card. If someone else is available, close your eyes and have them play 2nds, 3rds, 4ths, and 5ths on the keyboard for you and your child to identify. As an alternative, listen to the videos instead and ask children to point to the card that identifies each. Be sure that all of you know how to recognize all of these intervals before going on.

Review for a few minutes at a time until all of you can identify these sounds with confidence. There are a number of ways for you to play 5ths: C and G, D and A, E and B, F and C, G and D, and A and E.

Remember how you figured out the correct interval by eliminating incorrect intervals (songs)? Now you can add "Twinkle, Twinkle, Little Star" to the list of possibilities. That's the reason that I encouraged you to add only one new thing at a time. In fact, shortened titles could be sufficient for identification: "Birthday," "Bear," "Wheels," and "Twinkle." Often, children are so eager to demonstrate their new skill that it just takes too long to say the complete title!

MAJOR CHORDS

Chords support the melody and are the basis for harmony, which occurs in combinations of specific patterns built on sounds that you already know; you can demonstrate them for your children. The first chord we will learn is called a "C" chord. Its actual name is a "C major" chord, but usually, it is called just "C."

♪ MUSICAL ACTIVITY: C MAJOR CHORD

Using the same relaxed hand position, place your right hand with 1 on Middle C and 5 on G, with one finger on each white key. Can you play finger numbers 1, 3, and 5 (do, me, sol) individually, then all at once? Do not try to hold 2 and 4 up; just let them relax on the keys, as shown in the first part of Chapter 9. Which notes are you playing? That's right—C, E, and G.

Now it's time for your left hand to have a turn to play. Look at Middle C and the C below it. Using the same relaxed hand position, place your left hand so that 5 is on the low C and 1 is on the G above it, with one finger on each white key in between. Play finger numbers 5, 3, and 1 individually, then together. Again, be sure to relax 2 and 4. Congratulations—you have learned how to play a C chord with your right hand and your left hand!

Play C, E, and G one at a time, then together with your right hand, then your left. Say and sing the names of the notes; ask children to select the index cards with letters in the order used in the chord. If your child is still young, they can play notes one at a time using the supported hand position for children shown in Chapters 4 and 9. If their hands and fine motor coordination are advanced enough, they can begin to explore chords using the same hand position as shown for adults.

♪ MUSICAL ACTIVITY: G MAJOR CHORD

The next chord I would like to introduce to you is the G chord. Using the same relaxed hand position, place your right hand with 1 on G and 5 on D, with one finger on each white key. Can you play finger numbers 1, 3, and 5 all at once? Again, be sure to relax 2 and 4. Which notes are you playing? That's right—G, B, and D.

Now it's time for your left hand to have a turn to play. Look at the G below Middle C and the D just above it. Using the same relaxed hand position, place your left hand so that 5 is on G and 1 is on D above it, with one finger on each white key in between. Play finger numbers 5, 3, and 1 together. Ask children to select the index cards with letters in the order used in the chord.

Play G, B, and D one at a time, then together with your right hand, then your left. Say and sing the names of the notes; ask children to select the index cards with letters in the order used in the chord.

Now you have learned a C chord and a G chord. You also already know a song that uses those two chords: "The Wheels on the Bus." Would you like to play the harmony for it?

The melody begins with a G as a pickup note before the downbeat on C. The harmony begins and ends with a C chord. How will you know to change to a G chord? By how it sounds as you sing it. You will be able to tell when the C chord needs to be changed to a G chord. How do you know when to change back to a C chord? By how the melody goes; for this song, it works to change chords only on the downbeat. Figure out the next change to a G chord, and then you'll be ready to end with a C chord. There is a demonstration of the harmony on the Chapter 10 playlist for "C and G Chords."

MINOR CHORDS

Do you remember back in Chapter 3 when you experienced the downbeat? The examples included the outline of both a major and minor chord, and I introduced you to the difference by singing the sounds as well as exploring how music could be used to express emotion.

♪ MUSICAL ACTIVITY: A MINOR CHORD

Now it's time to learn more about a minor chord. Using the same relaxed hand position, place your right hand with 3 on Middle C, with one finger on each white key. In this position, 1 should be on the A below Middle C and 5 should be on E above Middle C. Can you play finger numbers 1, 3, and 5 individually, then all at once? Do not try to hold 2 and 4 up; just let them relax on the keys.

Now it's time to let your left hand play instead. Look at Middle C and the C below it. Using the same relaxed hand position, place your left hand so that 3 is on the low C and 1 is on the E above it, with one finger on each white key in between. Check to be sure that 5 is on A. Play finger numbers 5, 3, and 1 individually, then together. Again, be sure to relax 2 and 4. Say and sing the names of the notes; ask children to select the index cards with letters in the order used in the chord. Now you have learned how to play an A minor chord with your right hand and your left hand!

Does this chord sound different from C and G chords? The quality of the sound is not quite the same, is it? Congratulations—you have discovered how major and minor chords sound different from each other! Major chords have been described as bright or happy, while minor chords might be dark or sad. Perhaps each of you would like to describe them in a way that is meaningful to you individually.

CHORDS BUILT ON WHITE KEYS

Now that you know about two types of chords, it is time to explore the kinds of chords built on each white note. When you begin with A, you already know that it has a minor sound. Although B is next, it is a different kind of chord from major and minor, so we'll go on to C. Typically, major chords are not referred to as major unless another note is added. That's why you will see chords listed as C, F, and G, instead of C major, F major, and G major; however, minor chords are always called minor chords. In guitar music, an A minor chord would look like this: Am, with a lowercase "m."

♪ MUSICAL ACTIVITY:
CHORDS BUILT ON WHITE KEYS

Beginning with your right hand 3 on Middle C and one finger per white key, play 1 on A, 3 on C, and 5 on E together. Observe the minor sound. Next, play C, E, and G together. This is a major sound.

Take two index cards and print "MAJOR" on one and "MI-

NOR" on the other. Next, ask your child to close their eyes and listen while you play an A minor chord or a C major chord. Ask if the sound is major or minor. When they know the answer, they can hold up the corresponding card and say "major" or "minor." When all of you are able to recognize the difference easily, you are ready for the next step.

On the white keys, there are three major and three minor chords. Now we're going to explore which chords are major or minor. Remember not to use the chord with 1 on B. You've already explored A minor and C major.

The next note to build a chord is D, so place 1 on D, 3 on F, and 5 on A. Play them all together and listen to hear if it is major or minor. You can compare the sound to the A minor chord and the C major chord if you like. If you are thinking that the chord on D is minor, you are correct. Using the index cards with the names of the white keys along with the major and minor cards, ask your child to select the appropriate ones for the chord and put them together: say "D minor" as you play the chord again.

The next key to build a chord is E, so place 1 on E, 3 on G, and 5 on B. Play them all together and listen to hear if it is major or minor. You can compare the sound to the A minor chord and the C major chord if you like. If you are thinking that the chord on E is minor, you are correct. Using the index cards with the names of the white keys along with the major and minor cards, ask your child to select the appropriate ones for the chord and put them together: say "E minor" as you play the chord again.

The next note is F, so place 1 on F, 3 on A, and 5 on C. Play them all together and listen to hear if it is major or minor. You can compare the sound to the A minor chord and the C major chord if you like. If you are thinking that the chord on F is major, you are correct. Using the index cards with the names of the white keys along with the major and minor cards, ask your child to select the appropriate ones for the chord and put them together: say "F major" as you play the chord again.

The next chord is something you have already learned: the G major chord. Place 1 on G, 3 on B, and 5 on D. Play them all together and listen to hear the sound. Using the index cards with the names of the white keys along with the major and minor cards, ask your child to select the appropriate ones for the chord and put them together: say "G major" as you play the chord again.

Remember to review activities in the previous chapters. Here are some things you can do now with your children:

- Play, sing, and identify intervals: 2nd, 3rd, 4th, and 5th.
- Sing songs associated with each interval.
- Play a C chord and a G chord.
- Sing "The Wheels on the Bus" while playing the correct chord.
- Name the notes in each chord.
- Identify chords on the white keys (except B) as major or minor.

Now that you have learned how intervals sound both separately and together, would you like to see how they look? Let's continue to discover how to recognize the sounds you already know when you look at sheet music!

Chapter 11

Now that you know how intervals sound, you are ready to learn how to read intervals by using patterns. Plan to spend a little time five days a week on this process until all of you are familiar with these sounds. Short segments of less than 5 minutes are ideal; repeat often until all of you can identify intervals with confidence.

LINE AND SPACE NOTES

There are only two basic kinds of written notes: line and space notes. The line notes have a horizontal line going through the middle of them, and the space notes have horizontal lines going both above and below them.

Line and space notes

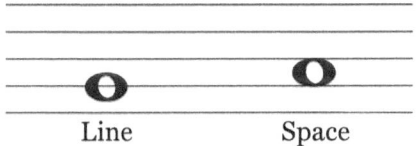

Line   Space

♪ MUSICAL ACTIVITY: LINE AND SPACE NOTES

Demonstrate a line note by holding your arm horizontally in front of your face, bent at the elbow, and straight from the elbow to the fingertips; your wrist should be in front of your eyes and most of your nose. The first picture represents a line note.

Line note representation

Next, demonstrate a space note by moving both arms in a similar fashion; however, this time, place your wrists parallel and directly over and under your head. This motion represents a space note.

Space note representation

Use index cards to make flash cards of line and space notes. Draw a circle on one card with one horizontal line through the middle. On a new card, draw another circle with two horizontal lines above and below it. Children can trace the line and space outlines with an index finger. Next, ask your child to make the appropriate signs with their arms to show line and space notes. Try taking turns and having them ask you to identify line and space notes by describing the position of the hands and making motions like the pictures. When this activity becomes easy, it is time to discover how to recognize intervals visually. Remember that you already know these sounds.

READING AND PLAYING INTERVALS: 2ND, 3RD, 4TH, AND 5TH

♪ MUSICAL ACTIVITY: READING AND PLAYING 2NDs (STEPS)

All intervals have patterns, and it is much easier if you know what to look for. When you see a 2nd, one note will always be a line note and the other a space note. Also, if you imagine sliding one note over another, one note would cover up part of the other. Beginning with your right thumb (1) on Middle C, play a 2nd up, down, and together as you look at this picture.

2nd or step

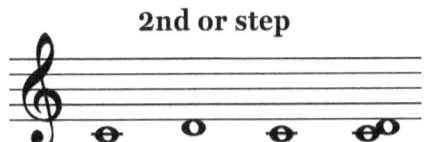

Congratulations—you have just played your first notes to written music! The most important part to understand is that these notes represent sounds that you have already learned.

Finally, take an index card and draw five horizontal, parallel lines on it. Add a short parallel line for Middle C like in the example. Now draw the notes, so that you can use them to identify what the sound of a 2nd looks like in notation. You don't have to worry about drawing the treble clef sign for flash cards to go with these examples. Just make sure that Middle C is on the lower part of the card. It may be easier to sketch first with a pencil and then trace with a marker. Next, ask children to trace with an index finger the up and down motion of the notes while saying "up" and "down" appropriately.

♪ MUSICAL ACTIVITY: READING AND PLAYING 3RDs (SKIPS)

The next interval after the 2nd is the 3rd (skip). This interval has notes that are all line or all space notes. If you slide the notes together, one will be just above the other, similar to a figure 8. With your right hand in the same position, play a 3rd up, down, and together as you look at this picture.

3rd or skip

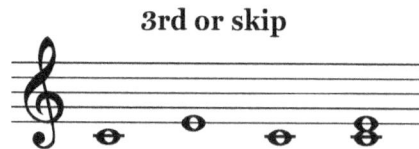

As you did previously, take an index card and draw five horizontal, parallel lines on it. Add a short parallel line for Middle C. Now draw notes just like the example, so that you can use them to identify what the sound of a 3rd looks like in notation. It may be easier to sketch first with a pencil and then trace with a marker. Next, ask children to trace the up and down motion of the notes while saying "up" and "down" appropriately.

♪ MUSICAL ACTIVITY: READING AND PLAYING 2NDs (STEPS) AND 3RDs (SKIPS)

Play a 2nd or a 3rd on the keyboard and match what you hear with what you see. Now look at the card and play what you see. Take turns with your child and continue until matches are correct almost all of the time.

Tip: remember that eliminating what something is not can be a useful part of the learning process. Ask if it sounds like "Happy Birthday" or "The Bear Went Over the Mountain."

♪ MUSICAL ACTIVITY: READING AND PLAYING 4THs

The next interval is a 4th and is a relative of a 2nd. The reason is that a 4th has both a line note and a space note. Which interval have you learned that has both types of notes? That's right, a 2nd. How can you tell the difference between a 2nd and a 4th? A 4th will have one horizontal line that doesn't go through either note. In contrast, remember that a 2nd (step) has no horizontal lines between the notes. Play a 4th up, down, and together as you look at this picture.

4th

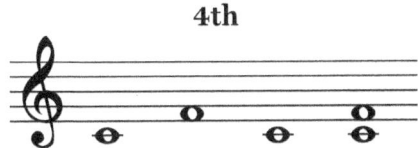

Once more, take an index card and draw five horizontal, parallel lines on it. Add a short parallel line for Middle C. Now draw notes just like the example, so that you can use them to identify what the sound of a 4th looks like in notation. It may be easier to sketch first with a pencil and then trace with a marker. Next, ask children to trace the up and down motion of the notes while saying "up" and "down" appropriately.

♪ MUSICAL ACTIVITY: READING AND PLAYING 2NDs (STEPS), 3RDs (SKIPS), AND 4THs

Play a 2nd, 3rd, or 4th on the keyboard and match what you hear with what you see on the flash cards. Now look at the card and play what you see. Take turns with your child and continue until matches are correct almost all of the time. Figure out which sounds match the songs you have learned and which sounds don't. Remember that repetition is the key to success with children.

Tip: remember that eliminating what something is not can be a useful part of the learning process. Ask if it sounds like "Happy Birthday," "The Bear Went Over the Mountain," or "The Wheels on the Bus."

♪ MUSICAL ACTIVITY: READING AND PLAYING 5THs

The next interval is a 5th and is a relative of a 3rd. This interval has notes that are all line or all space notes. If you imagine sliding the notes together, there will be a space just big enough for a note vertically between the notes of a 5th. Play a 5th up, down, and together as you look at this picture.

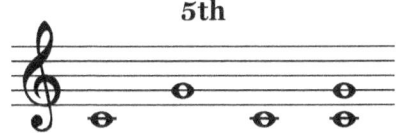

Congratulations—you did it! You played all of the intervals here from the written music, also called music notation! Again, take an index card and draw five horizontal, parallel lines on it. Add a short parallel line for Middle C. Now draw notes just like the example so that you can use them to identify what the sound of a 5th looks like in notation. It may be easier to sketch first with a pencil and then trace with a marker. Next, ask children to trace the up and down motion of the notes while saying "up" and "down" appropriately.

♪ MUSICAL ACTIVITY: READING AND PLAYING 2NDs (STEPS), 3RDs (SKIPS), 4THs, AND 5THs

Play a 2nd, 3rd, 4th, or 5th on the keyboard and match what you hear with what you see on the index cards. Now look at the card and play what you see. Take turns with children and continue until matches are correct almost all of the time. Compare the sounds with the beginnings of "Happy Birthday," "The Bear Went Over the Mountain," "The Wheels on the Bus," and "Twinkle, Twinkle Little Star." It really does become easier with experience.

♪ MUSICAL ACTIVITY: DUET PRACTICE

In order to play successfully with someone else, both players must feel the same rhythm so that the music starts and ends at the same time and stays together in the middle. No one wins if anyone finishes first, but all must finish together to succeed. This accomplishment is one of the reasons that playing successfully with a group demonstrates teamwork to a potential employer.

When I was a faculty member at a university, I taught every student in my classes to play a simple piece on a portable keyboard using both hands (not at the same time). Recording their successes to share with family and friends was one of my favorite parts of the course! As long as you have normal structure and function of nerves and muscles in your upper body, you can learn this piece, too.

The first thing to learn is the rhythm of a piece that I like to call "Chocolates." You have already learned this rhythmic pattern, so remember to say it in three syllables. The actual sheet music is in Suggested Reading by Camp.

The reason it is called "Chocolates" is that by simply repeating "*CHOC*olate" eight times, you will have the rhythm of the entire piece. With one step on the downbeat each time, step and clap "*CHOC*olate" eight times.

Now we need a new hand position to play all of those sounds in order. The musical name for these patterns is the diatonic (DY uh tahn ic) scale. Using a relaxed hand position, place your left pinky (5) on Middle C and your right pinky (5) on the next C up the keyboard. Let your thumbs hang off and make sure that you have one finger for each white key as shown in this example:

Hand position for "*CHOC*olates"

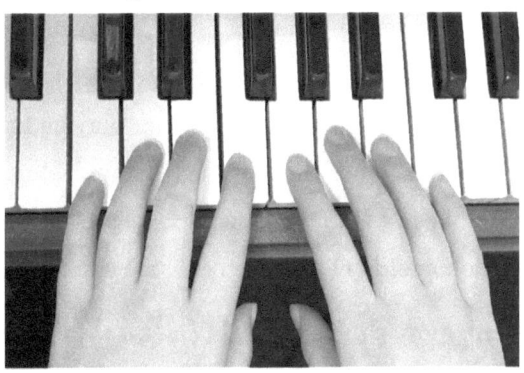

Go to the Chapter 11 playlist for "Chocolates" on my website, DrJaneJBader.com/chapter-videos. Sing or say "*CHOC*olate" with the example. Next, try playing along with it.

Sometimes, videos are removed from YouTube, so if you find that one is missing, please send an email to me at Jane@ DrJaneJBader.com with the subject line "Missing Video." It would help if you could also include the title and chapter number of the missing video so that I can select an alternative. I would really appreciate it!

♪ MUSICAL ACTIVITY: DUET PERFORMANCE

When you play it easily, it is time to play the duet (doo ET): two performers playing one piece together. You are ready to play the melody, while I play the harmony (accompaniment). We'll repeat it once, so go back to the beginning while keeping a steady beat. I'll play an introduction of two "*CHOC*olates." Go to the last item on the playlist for Chapter 11 to play along with "Duet for Chocolates."

If you are playing with another person at your keyboard, you will need to move your hand position up eight notes. First, move your hand position so that your left pinky (5) is where your right pinky was and your right pinky is on the next C up the keyboard. The reason is that if two people are playing at the same keyboard, there has to be room for the person playing the lower part. If you're playing with the video, use whatever position you like. In fact, you could try both to see which you like better.

Here are some more things that you can do with your children now:

- Recognize the difference between line and space notes.
- Read intervals: 2nd, 3rd, 4th, and 5th.
- Play intervals: 2nd, 3rd, 4th, and 5th.
- Learn, practice, and perform "Chocolates."
- Perform the "Duet for Chocolates" with the video.

Wasn't that great fun? I am so proud of all of you for participating in learning musical concepts. Parents and other caregivers, you have helped nurture your children's brain development and given them a foundation for learning more about music. If you or your children decide to pursue further music study, it could be enormously easier because of this foundation. As children grow older and their memory retains concepts longer, reviewing activities in this book can be done weekly to monthly. If your child should want to join the band, orchestra, or chorus, this knowledge and experience will serve them well in all of their future musical endeavors. Congratulations—you made it all the way through and deserve to celebrate your magnificent accomplishment!

CONCLUSION

Do you remember that I described how music provided an enjoyable part-time job for our daughter as a teenager? In addition to playing violin for weddings, she also played background piano music for social functions, particularly at retirement centers. Although we encouraged and supported her all the way, her success was self-motivated. As a reminder from Chapter 1, one of the benefits of music study is that numerous life skills are developed during the process, including academic, social, physical, and personal development.

Our daughter set goals for herself, practiced regularly, and prepared well for auditions (graded performances for judges). In addition to being a member of All-State Orchestra from sixth grade through high school, she wanted to attend an orchestra camp one summer, so she earned a scholarship by audition. Her next goal was to attend the Governor's School summer program in violin, which she accomplished again by audition. During her senior year in high school, she won first prize in the concerto competition for the youth orchestra in piano. As a result, she had the unique privilege of performing a piano piece accompanied by an orchestra of her friends.

What did our daughter do after high school? Believe it or not, she earned a Bachelor of Science Degree in Entomology (insects). As a freshman, she earned one music and three academic scholarships. Since she was a toddler, she has been fascinated by bugs. She developed her eye-hand coordination before she was 2 years old by quickly—but gently—catching crickets as they jumped in the grass. We encouraged and supported her interest in bugs all the way, too, even though we sometimes may have learned more than we really wanted to know. We even took her over twenty-five miles one way to a state park, where she regularly volunteered as an assistant naturalist from fifth grade through high school.

What did our daughter do after college? She continued to play violin in an orchestra and rear insects in a lab until she had her own children; then, she taught violin as well as community classes about bugs. Later, she earned a Master's in Library and Information Science, becoming a Science Librarian at a large state university. Because we had played together and shared music so much while she was growing up, one of my favorite things to do at Christmas is to play piano duets with her. Consequently, she is an excellent example of how music can provide learning experiences and rewards throughout childhood, with benefits extending well into adulthood.

In this book, you have learned how to feel the downbeat and why it is important, how to recognize rhythmic patterns, and how to figure out songs to help you hear and play melodies. You've discovered the value of repetition and review in learning, how musical preferences are developed, how to find opportunities for attending performances, and how music can promote brain development and shape children's futures in a positive way. It was a new experience to learn how to shop for a keyboard and to explore how it is oriented, along with learning the sounds and names of notes and how to navigate the keyboard.

After you began this musical journey, you listened to examples and picked out tunes on the keyboard with a little guidance. How cool was that? Next, you taught your children important musical concepts related to words already in their vocabulary, expanding to include pitch, dynamics, tempo, articulation, and timbre before launching into creative music making.

After learning the names of neighbor groups of keys, you matched the sounds of songs that you already knew with musical distances. Next, you explored finger numbers, hand positions, and visual elements of making music (such as the treble and bass clefs), as well as intervals. Finally, you reached the culmination of playing a simple piece with both hands, one after the other. Playing "Chocolates" with a duet part as an accompaniment is a crowning achievement for all of you that deserves to be shared and celebrated with your friends and family!

You have gone way outside your comfort zone and been willing to make mistakes, but then you have figured out what happened and how to fix it. You have taken your family on a new musical adventure, guided by the roadmap in this book. It takes courage to dive into a new subject in a nontraditional way, in which you learn along with your children.

Are you surprised by how much all of you have accomplished? I knew you could do it! I have enjoyed this musical journey with you enormously and wish it could have been in person.

If any of you wants to study music further, there is more information listed on my website, DrJaneJBader.com/Resources, under Additional Websites. One organization is the Music Teachers National Association (MTNA), and they have a referral system to locate a music teacher in your area. Another organization to look up is the Suzuki Association of the Americas. Their teachers can begin teaching violin and other instruments to students as young as 3 years old. If there is a pedagogy (PED uh go jee) professor or department in your area, you might ask about students who teach with periodic observations by professors, sometimes referred to as practice teaching. Church musicians and school musicians, as well as friends, could also offer word-of-mouth recommendations.

If you're a music teacher, I have content especially for you on my website, DrJaneJBader.com/Resources. Please visit it to learn more about hearing protection, suggested reading, and additional websites. For those of you who have asked about my earlier research, there is a link to my dissertation in Suggested Reading under Bader. Thank you for your interest!

The activities in this book are designed to be enjoyed through the first five years of a child's life. By spending time with your children studying music, you can enhance their brain development and provide enrichment that can benefit them for the rest of their life.

I would love to know about your musical journey, so please share it with me at Jane@DrJaneJBader.com. Some of you will have questions, so please send an email to the same address. I plan to include additional FAQs from the community on my website in the future. For more information or to contact me about online groups, workshops, podcasts, speaking engagements, and materials for music teachers, please visit my website, DrJaneJBader.com. Be sure to check for updates and new posts.

Thank you for allowing me to share a subject I truly love. I fervently hope that you have enjoyed your time of discovering musical concepts and exploring the keyboard and that all of you will enjoy music every day of your life!

ACKNOWLEDGMENTS

It took the support of many for me to succeed in my career to the point that I could write this book, and there are simply no words to adequately express my profound gratitude to the following people:

First, my late mother and father. They instilled in me the desire for learning and worked hard to provide a piano and lessons, plus transportation. Also, they modeled a strong work ethic that enabled them to overcome numerous obstacles, including poverty, and enjoy successful careers.

My family, to whom this book is dedicated. Each person played a special part:

My husband, Mike Bader, who grocery shopped, cooked delicious meals, and washed lots of dishes—in addition to proofreading everything and listening to the read-aloud edit before the final iteration. He also provided valuable assistance with still and video photography.

Our daughter, Karen Bader Burton, who gave feedback on organization and presentation of content and helped with editing, proofreading, and extensive tech support, as well as sharing generously her expertise in information science.

Our son-in-law, James Daly Burton, who volunteered to help as my IT consultant and enabled me to save money on software.

Our granddaughter, Joyce Elizabeth Burton, who contributed some of her drawings as an award-winning artist, as well as her knowledge of Google Drive and uploading graphics.

Our granddaughter, Marie Catherine Burton, who contributed some of her work, specifically with digital graphics and still photography, as an award-winning artist.

Our grandson, Xavier Vincent Burton, who provided the perfect example for the demonstration of musical concepts in videos.

Our son-in-law's mother (my co-mother-in-law) and our friend, Mary Ann Wheeler, who volunteered to be a beta reader and provided valuable feedback.

Our son-in-law's father and our friend, Frederick Earl Burton III, who assisted in providing backgrounds for photos and videos.

Dr. Stephen Zdzinski, my dissertation director, who valued and guided my research—as well as encouraged me along the final steps to earning a doctoral degree, particularly in navigating the academic minefield.

Dr. William Bates, who recommended a superb director for my dissertation and approved the course documentation required for graduation.

Dr. Stephen Taylor, a pedagogy professor, colleague, friend, and our daughter's piano teacher, without whose encouragement and support I could not have earned my doctorate.

The late Dr. Max Camp, who observed prodigies and analyzed their mental processes involved in learning to play a piano piece. He taught comprehensive pedagogy that I have applied successfully to homeschooling as well as teaching piano and music.

Dr. Georgia Cowart, who provided inspiration and set a wonderful example of a multisensory approach to learning.

Dr. Gordon (Dick) Goodwin, who encouraged me to compose music and helped me to overcome significant obstacles along the path to a doctorate.

Dr. Reginald Bain, who opened up to me the world of computers in music and encouraged me to compose in different ways.

The late Professor W. John Williams, who always made piano lessons incredibly interesting as well as thoroughly enjoyable.

Dr. Mary Lynne Bennett, who analyzed different methods of teaching piano for my research on sequencing aural skills in elementary piano students.

Dr. Stephen Cook, whose performances at master class of Beethoven's Piano Sonata, Op. 53, enabled me to answer correctly during my oral doctoral comprehensive examinations when I was asked in what key the second theme of the first movement was written.

The late Dr. Fred Teuber, after whose class I became an award-winning composer.

Dr. Jerry Curry, who considered my minor in math a perfectly acceptable choice for the equivalent of an undergraduate degree with a major in music.

Dr. Marina Lomazov and Dr. Joseph Rackers, who founded and brought the Southeastern Piano Festival to the University of South Carolina.

Nick Luby and Susan Zhang, who expanded access to piano performance through The Concert Truck.

Dr. Nick Ruggiero, who inspired me to share my knowledge and experience because of his desire to have his children study music.

Dr. Carolyn Joy Wilson, who earned a doctorate over the same period of time as I did, whose help and support made it possible for both of us to finish in the same year.

Other friends, including Dr. Ann B. Wilson, Dr. Robert Jones, Johanna Wilson, Pat Cannon, and Marty Jones, who supported, encouraged, and prayed for me during the entire process.

My wonderful colleagues at the Columbia Music Teachers Association, who kindly invited me to share my research and received it graciously. Dr. Bonny Miller (bonnymillermusic.com) and Dr. Myungsook Stoudenmire were particularly helpful and supportive of this book.

Online marketing classmate Lucia da Vinci, whose insight and encouragement helped me to reduce stress while learning and figure out how to communicate more effectively.

Dr. David Cutler, who planted the idea of writing a book during a session at the Southeastern Piano Festival.

Marty Fort, author of *The Ultimate Guide To Music Lessons: For Parents, Students or Anyone Who's Ready to Play Music!*, whose book inspired me to ask myself how I could provide learning experiences for musical concepts as a natural part of growth and development during the years before music lessons are even considered.

Fellow authors, who helped me through rough spots and provided direction and encouragement:

James Baker, author of *Live Forever & Fix Everything* (liveforeverfixeverything.com)

Bill Buvens, author (cancerfreeblueprint.com)

Edward Conley, author of *Promote the Dog Sitter* (edwardconley.com)

Mary Guirovich, author of *God's Not Done with You* (maryguirovich.com)

William Krause, author of *Unlearning Addiction* (williamkrause.com)

Dr. Cori Lathan, author of *Inventing the Future* (inventthefuture.tech).

I want to thank each one of the following special people who combined their numerous skills to support my journey as an author. Some provided editorial perspective along with reassurance that I was on the right path. All lent their support and skills to keep this book on track, and my book would not have been possible without all of these writing and publishing specialists:

Hussein Al-Baiaty (Founder of Rising Authors and Community Manager) www.husseinalbaiaty.com

Miles Rote (Author Strategist)

Rikki Jump (Author Strategy Lead)

Kathleen McIntosh (Editor)

Skyler Gray (Editor and Book Title)

Jennifer Baxter (Digital Marketing Manager) jenbaxter.com

Carmela Wright (Multimedia Marketing Specialist)

Miranda Talbert (Website Assistant)

Alexa Davis (Website Designer) alexamariedavis.com

Tucker Max (Online Workshop Leader)

Hal Clifford (Editor in Chief) halclifford.com

Emily Gindlesparger (Head Book Coach) depthfinder.work

Chas Hoppe (Founder, Cape and Cowl Media) capeandcowlmedia.com

Eliece Pool (Author Success Manager)

Katie Orr (Author Success Manager)

Emily Anderson (Author Success Manager)

Meghan McCracken (Chief Experience Officer)

Vanessa Restifo (Project Manager)

Benito Salazar (Project Manager)

Sheila Parr (Cover Designer) www.sheilaparr.com

John van der Woude (Imprint Designer), JVDW Designs,
    jvdwdesigns.com

Erin Michelle Sky (Back Cover Copy)

Laura Cail (Quality Assurance) www.wordshavewings.biz

Leslie Wilson (Quality Assurance and Proofreading)

Braxton Benes (Quality Assurance and Production)

Ellie Cole (Head of Author Success)

Sophie May (Author Experience Coach)

Drew Applebaum (Earlier Community Manager)

Mary Horn (Executive Assistant)

Jen Kallas (Digital Marketing)

Rose Friel (Publishing Consultant & Creative Matchmaker)
    www.forewordlitconsulting.com

Anastasia Voll (Final Proofreading and Copyediting/Quality
    Assurance) www.vollcontentmarketing.com

Jesse Sussman (Marketing, Publishing, and Website)
    www.fullwellmedia.com

Suggested Reading

Please visit DrJaneJBader.com/Resources to view
the growing list of recommended resources.

Altenmüller, Eckart, Stanley Finger, and Francois Boller, eds. *Music, Neurology, and Neuroscience: Historical Connections and Perspectives*. Elsevier, 2015.

Anvari, Sima H., Laurel Trainor, Jennifer Woodside, and Betty Ann Levy. "Relations Among Musical Skills, Phonological Processing, and Early Reading Ability in Preschool Children." *Journal of Experimental Child Psychology* 83, no. 2 (October 2002): 111-130.

Bader, Jane Jones. "Sequencing Aural Skills in Elementary Piano Literature." DMA diss., University of South Carolina, 2001.

Bahnson, Frederic. *Better Than Destiny: Practical Science for Creating the Life You Want*. Austin, TX: Lioncrest Publishing, 2021.

Baker, Mitzi. "Music Moves Brain To Pay Attention, Stanford Study Finds." *news release, Stanford School of Medicine*, http://med.stanford.edu/news_releases/2007/july/music.html 16 (2007).

Bevill, Kim. *Top Ten Things: The Neuroscience on Sex Differences, Music, Gaming and More*. n.p.: Balboa Press, 2021.

Bilhartz, Terry, Rick Bruhn, and Judith Olson. "The Effect of Early Music Training on Child Cognitive Development." *Journal of Applied Developmental Psychology* 20, no. 4 (1999): 615-636.

Blanchard, Keith. *Reverberation: Do Everything Better with Music*. New York: Harry N. Abrams, 2023.

Bloom, Benjamin. *Developing Talent in Young People*. New York: Ballantine Books, 1985.

Bugaj, Katarzyna, and Brenda Brenner. "The Effects of Music Instruction on Cognitive Development and Reading Skills—An Overview." *Bulletin of the Council for Research in Music Education* 189 (2011): 89-104.

Burnett, William, and David J. Evans. *Designing Your Life*. New York: Alfred A. Knopf, 2016.

Butzlaff, Ron. "Can Music Be Used to Teach Reading?" *Journal of Aesthetic Education* 34, no. 3/4 (2000): 167-78.

Camp, Max W. *Developing Piano Performance: A Teaching Philosophy*. Chapel Hill, NC: Hinshaw Music, 1981, p. 57.

Camp, Max W. *Teaching Piano: The Synthesis of Mind, Ear and Body*. Los Angeles, CA: Alfred Publishing Co., Inc., 1992, p.55.

Cassidy, Jane W., and Donald R. Speer. "Music Terminology: A Transfer from Knowledge to Practical Use." *Bulletin of the Council for Research in Music Education* 106 (Fall,1990): 11-21.

Chao-Fernández, Rocío, Sara Román-García, and Aurelio Chao-Fernández. "Art, Science and Magic: Music and Math the Classroom." In *Proceedings of the 5th International Conference on Technological Ecosystems for Enhancing Multiculturality*, pp. 1-5. 2017.

Collins, Anita. "Neuroscience Meets Music Education: Exploring the Implications of Neural Processing Models on Music Education Practice." *International Journal of Music Education* 31, no.2 (2013): 217-231.

Condello, Robert Anthony. *Effects of Sequencing on Meaningful Learning*. Hofstra University, 1975.

Cook, Stephen. "Through The Eyes Of a Child: Pianistic Paths For The Smallest Learners." *American Music Teacher* 66, no.6 (2017): 10-13.

Cranmore, Jeff, and Jeanne Tunks. "Brain Research on the Study of Music and Mathematics: A Meta-Synthesis." *Journal of Mathematics Education* 8, no. 2 (2015): 139-157.

Ellenberger, Carl. *Theme and Variations: Musical Notes by a Neurologist.* n.p.: Promusica Press, 2019.

Fernandez, Sabrina. "Music and Brain Development." *Pediatric Annals* 47, no. 8 (2018): e306-e308.

Flowers, Patricia J. "The Effect of Instruction in Vocabulary and Listening on Nonmusicians' Descriptions of Changes in Music." *Journal of Research in Music Education* 31, no. 3 (1983): 179-189.

Flowers, Patricia J. "Music Vocabulary of First-Grade Children: Words Listed for Instruction and their Actual Use." *Journal of Research in Music Education* 46, no. 1 (1998): 5-15.

Fort, Marty. *The Ultimate Guide to Music Lessons: For Parents, Students, or Anyone Who's Ready to Play Music!* Little Rock, AR: Expert Press, 2018.

Gamble, Denise Kath. *A Study of the Effects of Two Types of Tonal Pattern Instruction on the Audiational and Performance Skills of First-Year Clarinet Students.* Temple University, 1989.

Granier-Deferre, Carolyn, Sophie Bassereau, Aurélie Ribeiro, Anne-Yvonne Jacquet, and Anthony J. DeCasper. "A Melodic Contour Repeatedly Experienced by Human Near-Term Fetuses Elicits a Profound Cardiac Reaction One Month after Birth." *PLoS One* 6, no. 2 (2011): e17304.

Grutzmacher, Patricia Ann. "The Effect of Tonal Pattern Training on the Aural Perception, Reading Recognition, and Melodic Sightreading Achievement of First-Year Instrumental Music Students." *Journal of Research in Music Education* 35 (1987): 171-181.

Hair, Harriet I. "Discrimination of Tonal Direction on Verbal and Nonverbal Tasks by First Grade Children." *Journal of Research in Music Education* 25 (1977): 197-210.

Hallam, Susan. "The Power of Music: Its Impact on the Intellectual, Social and Personal Development of Children and Young People." *International Journal of Music Education* 28, no. 3 (2010): 269-289.

Hamilton, Tara Julia, Julieanne Doai, Andrew Milne, Vicky Saisanas, Andrea Calilhanna, Courtney Hilton, Micah Goldwater, and Richard Cohn. "Teaching Mathematics with Music: A Pilot Study." In *2018 IEEE International Conference on Teaching, Assessment, and Learning for Engineering (TALE)*, pp. 927-931. IEEE, 2018.

Hannon, Erin E., and Laurel J. Trainor. "Music Acquisition: Effects of Enculturation and Formal Training on Development." *Trends in Cognitive Sciences* 11, no. 11 (2007), 466-472.

Helding, Lynn. *The Musician's Mind: Teaching, Learning, and Performance in the Age of Brain Science*. Washington, DC: Rowman & Littlefield Publishers, 2020.

Hepper, Peter G. "An Examination of Fetal Learning Before and After Birth." *The Irish Journal of Psychology* 12, no. 2 (1991): 95-107.

Hersch, Sarah Smith. *Music Educator Shinichi Suzuki: His Teacher Development Program and Studio Teaching*. University of Minnesota, 1995.

Hodges, Donald A. "Implication of Music and Brain Research: This introductory article offers an overview of neuromusical research and articulates some basic premises derived from this research." *Music Educators Journal* 87, no. 2 (2000): 17-22.

Hodges, Donald A. "The Child Musician's Brain." *The Child as Musician: A Handbook of Musical Development* (2015): 52-66.

Houser, Larry Lee. *Toward a Theory of Sequencing: Study (2, 3)-1: An Exploration of the Effects of Three Instructional Sequences on Achievement of Selected Instructional Objectives in Conversion of Units in the Metric System of Measure*. The Pennsylvania State University, 1974.

Hyde, Krista L., Jason Lerch, Andrea Norton, Marie Forgeard, Ellen Winner, Alan C. Evans, and Gottfried Schlaug. "Musical Training Shapes Structural Brain Development." *Journal of Neuroscience* 29, no. 10 (2009): 3019-3025.

Johansson, Barbro B. "Music, Age, Performance, and Excellence: A Neuroscientific Approach." *Psychomusicology: A Journal of Research in Music Cognition* 18, no. 1-2 (2002): 46.

Johansson, Barbro B. "Music and Brain Plasticity." *European Review* 14, no. 1 (2006), 49-64.

Kells, Deanne. "The Impact of Music on Mathematics Achievement." Accessed January 6, 2022. http://www.microtonemusic.net/ About_Microtone_Music/Expert_Research/Benefits_of_ Kindermusik/ImpactOfMusicOnMath.pdf

Küpana, M. Nevra. "Social Emotional Learning and Music Education." *SED-Sanat Eğitimi Dergisi* 3, no. 1 (2015): 75-88.

Leipold, Simon, Carina Klein, and Lutz Jancke. "Musical Expertise Shapes Functional and Structural Brains Network Independent of Absolute Pitch Ability." *Journal of Neuroscience* 41, no. 11 (2021): 2496-2511.

Levitin, Daniel. *This is your Brain on Music: The Science of a Human Obsession.* New York: Plume/Penguin, 2007.

Mannone, Maria, and Luca Turchet. "Shall We (Math and) Dance?" In *Mathematics and Computation in Music: 7th International Conference, MCM 2019*, Madrid, Spain, June 18-21, 2019, Proceedings 7 (pp. 84-97). Springer International Publishing.

Marcus, Gary. *Guitar Zero: The New Musicians and the Science of Learning.* London: Penguin Press, 2012.

Marzano, Robert J. and Daisy E. Arredondo. "Restructuring Schools Through the Teaching of Thinking Skills." *Educational Leadership*, 43, no. 8 (1986): 20-26.

McPherson, Gary E., Peter Miksza, and Paul Evans. "Self-Regulated Learning in Music Practice and Performance." In *Handbook of Self-Regulation of Learning and Performance*, pp. 181-193. Routledge, 2017.

Miendlarzewska, Ewa, and Wiebke J. Frost. "How Musical Training Affects Cognitive Development: Rhythm, Reward, and Other Modulating Variables." *Frontiers in Neuroscience* 7 (2014): 279.

Moreno, Sylvain, Ellen Bialystok, Raluca Barac, E. Glenn Schellenberg, Nicholas, J. Cepeda, and Tom Chau. "Short-Term Music Training Enhances Verbal Intelligence and Executive Function." *Psychological Science* 22, no. 11 (2011): 1425-1433.

Nazzi, Thierry, Caroline Floccia, and Josiane Bertoncini. "Discrimination of Pitch Contours by Neonates." *Infant Behavior and Development* 21, no. 4 (1998): 779-784.

Nyberg, Lars, Reza Habib, Anthony R. McIntosh, and Endel Tulving. "Reactivation of Encoding-Related Brain Activity during Memory Retrieval." *Proceedings of the National Academy of Sciences* 97, no. 20 (2000): 11120-11124.

Patel, Aniruddh D. *Music, Language, and the Brain.* 1st ed. Oxford University Press, 2010.

Peretz, Isabelle, and Robert Zatorre. "Brain Organization for Music Processing." *Annual Review of Psychology* 56, no. 1 (2005): 89-114.

Peretz, Isabelle, and Robert J. Zatorre, eds. *The Cognitive Neuroscience of Music.* Oxford University Press, 2003.

Phillips-Silver, Jessica. "On the Meaning of Movement in Music, Development and the Brain." *Contemporary Music Review* 28, no. 3 (2009): 293-314.

Robinson, Jerry W. and T. James Crawford. "Fundamental Considerations in Sequencing and Teaching Basic Typing Applications." *Balance Sheet* 60, no. 1 (1978): 4-7.

Rodriguez, Carlos X. "Children's Perception, Production, and Description of Musical Expression." *Journal of Research in Music Education* 46, no. 1 (1998): 48-61.

Sacks, Oliver. *Musicophilia: Tales of Music and the Brain.* New York: Vintage Books, 2008.

Schlaug, Gottfried, Andrea Norton, Katie Overy, and Ellen Winner. "Effects of Music Training on the Child's Brain and Cognitive Development." *Annals of the New York Academy of Sciences* 1060, no. 1 (2006): 219-230. https://doi.org/10.1196/annals.1360.015

Schlaug, Gottfried, Lutz Jäncke, Yanxiong Huang, Jochen F. Staiger, and Helmuth Steinmetz. "Increased Corpus Callosum Size in Musicians." *Neuropsychologia* 33, no. 8 (1995): 1047-1055.

Scott-Kassner, Carol. "Developing Teachers for Early Childhood Programs: Research about the Impact of Music on Brain Development Highlights the Need to Prepare Teachers to Provide Effective Music Instruction in Day-Care Preschool Settings." *Music Educators Journal* 86, no. 1 (1999): 19-25.

Scripp, Larry. "An Overview of Research on Music and Learning." *Critical Links: Learning in the Arts and Student Academic and Social Development* (2002): 132-136.

Speranza, Luisa, Salvatore Pulcrano, Carla Perrone-Capano, Umberto di Porzio, and Floriana Volpicelli. "Music Affects Functional Brain Connectivity and Is Effective in the Treatment of Neurological Disorders." *Reviews in the Neurosciences* 33, no. 7 (2022): 789-801.

Strait, Dana L., Jane Hornickel, and Nina Kraus. "Subcortical Processing of Speech Regularities Predicts Reading and Music Aptitude in Children." *Behavioral and Brain Functions* 7 (2011): 1-11.

Sherman, Larry S., and Dennis Plies. *Every Brain Needs Music: The Neuroscience of Making and Listening to Music*. New York: Columbia University Press, 2023.

Sulzer, David. *Music, Math, and Mind: The Physics and Neuroscience of Music*. New York: Columbia University Press, 2021.

Svard, Lois. *The Musical Brain: What Students, Teachers, and Performers Need to Know*. Oxford University Press, 2023.

Teachout, David J. "The Impact of Music Education on a Child's Growth and Development." *Sounds of Learning*. Carlsbad, CA: International Foundation for Music Research (2005).

Thaut, Michael H. *Rhythm, Music, and the Brain: Scientific Foundations and Clinical Applications*. Taylor & Francis, 2013.

Thaut, Michael H., and Donald A. Hodges, eds. *The Oxford Handbook of Music and the Brain*. Oxford University Press, 2019.

Trainor, Laurel J, Céline Marie, David Gerry, Elaine Whiskin, and Andrea Unrau. "Becoming Musically Enculturated: Effects of Music Classes for Infants on Brain and Behavior." *Annals of the New York Academy of Sciences* 1252, no. 1 (2012): 129-138.

Ullman, M. "Music and Language Are Processed by The Same Brain Systems." *Neuroimage Georgetown University Medical Center* (2007). Accessed March 21, 2021. www.sciencedaily.com/releases/2007/09/07092712110.htm.

Van Der Schyff, Dylan, Andrea Schiavio, and David J. Elliott. *Musical Bodies, Musical Minds: Inactive Cognitive Science and the Meaning of Human Musicality*. MIT Press, 2022.

Virtala, Paula, Minna Huotilainen, Eino Partanen, Vineta Vellman, and Mari Tervaniemi. "Newborn Infants' Auditory System Is Sensitive to Western Music Chord Categories." *Frontiers in Psychology* 4 (2013): 492.

Wheeler, Mark E., Steven E. Petersen, and Randy L. Buckner. "Memory's Echo: Vivid Remembering Reactivates Sensory-Specific Cortex." *Proceedings of the National Academy of Sciences* 97, no. 20 (2000): 11125-11129.

White-Schwoch, Travis, Kali Woodruff Carr, Samira Anderson, Dana L. Strait, and Nina Kraus. "Older Adults Benefit from Music Training Early in Life: Biological Evidence for Long-Term Training-Driven Plasticity." *Journal of Neuroscience* 33, no. 45 (2013): 17667-17674.

Williamson, Victoria. *You Are The Music: How Music Reveals What It Means To Be Human*. London: Icon Books Ltd, 2014.

Winkler, István, Gábor P. Háden, Olivia Ladinig, István Sziller, and Henkjan Joning. "Newborn Infants Detect the Beat in Music." *Proceedings of the National Academy of Sciences* USA 106, no. 7 (2009): 2468-2471.

Zatorre, Robert. *From Perception to Pleasure: The Neuroscience of Music and Why We Love It.* Oxford University Press, 2023.

Zimmerman, Emily, and Amir Lahav. "The Multisensory Brain and Its Ability to Learn Music." *Annals of the New York Academy of Sciences* 1252, no. 1 (2012), 179-184.

Zimmerman, Marilyn P. "Musical Characteristics of Children." Washington, DC: Music Educators National Conference, 1971.

Zuk, Jennifer, Christopher Benjamin, Arnold Kenyon, and Nadine Gaab. "Behavioral and Neural Correlates of Executive Functioning in Musicians and Non-Musicians." *PLoS One* 9, no.6 (2014): e99868.

About the Author

Jane J. Bader, DMA, didn't set out to be a music teacher. Her first job was actually as a computer programmer. In her first career, she performed research in marine biology, conducted routine testing in a blood bank in Alaska, and orchestrated the ins and outs of a medical laboratory thanks to a Bachelor of Science in Cell Biology and a Certificate and Registration in Medical Technology. She also managed a clinical laboratory, where she taught student assistants as well as family practice residents how to perform basic lab tests accurately in order to diagnose and treat illnesses.

After their daughter was born, Dr. Bader and her husband discovered that she had neglected to read the baby book that said babies are supposed to sleep and take naps. Consequently, it was time to turn her hobby into a career, and she began arranging and composing music for local churches.

After becoming an award-winning composer, she earned a Master of Music and Doctor of Musical Arts in piano pedagogy and started teaching at a local university. Her ultimate performance opportunity occurred during a family trip to Las Vegas when she was asked to play Liberace's pianos at his museum, both the concert grand covered in mirrored rectangles and the studio grand in Swarovski crystals. Despite the impromptu performance, the audience enjoyed it so much that they even invited her back! The next time, she composed and arranged music to showcase the unique characteristics of his famous pianos.

Dr. Bader loves teaching and has taught chemistry, biology, math, typing, AP music theory, and an introduction to art, music, architecture, and ballet, in addition to the subjects necessary for homeschooling until their daughter became a university student. She wrote *Music for the Developing Brain* to help parents and caregivers everywhere share music with their children from the very beginning, so that they can enhance their children's brain development through music study—even if they've never had a music lesson in their life!

Dr. Bader previously lived in Alaska, Arizona, and Texas, and she has resided in South Carolina with her husband for decades. Her favorite people to visit are their daughter and son-in-law and their three children, where there is never a dull moment. In addition to teaching, playing the piano, and writing music, Dr. Bader enjoys traveling, reading, and visiting museums.

Dr. Bader is passionate about sparking joy for people by making music a collaborative and fun experience. She would love to know about your musical journey, so please remember to share it with her at Jane@DrJaneJBader.com. Some of you will have questions, so please send an email to the same address. She plans to include additional FAQs from the community on her website in the future. For more information or to contact her for workshops or speaking engagements, please visit her website, DrJaneJBader.com.

www.ingramcontent.com/pod-product-compliance
Lightning Source LLC
Chambersburg PA
CBHW020255130626
46549CB00005B/2223